INTRODUCING
ISSUES WITH
OPPOSING
VIEWPOINTS®

Gun
Control

Other books in the Introducing Issues
with Opposing Viewpoints series:

INTRODUCING
ISSUES WITH
OPPOSING
VIEWPOINTS®

Gun Control

Beth Rosenthal, *Book Editor*

Christine Nasso, *Publisher*
Elizabeth Des Chenes, *Managing Editor*

GREENHAVEN PRESS
An imprint of Thomson Gale, a part of The Thomson Corporation

THOMSON
™
GALE

Detroit • New York • San Francisco • New Haven, Conn. • Waterville, Maine • London

LIBRARY OF CONGRESS CATALOGING-IN-PUBLICATION DATA

Gun control / Beth Rosenthal, book editor.
    p. cm. — (Introducing issues with opposing viewpoints)
    Includes bibliographical references and index.
    ISBN-13: 978-0-7377-3597-0 (hardcover)
    ISBN-10: 0-7377-3597-X (hardcover)
    1. Gun control—United States. 2. Firearms ownership—United States. 3. Violence—United States. I. Rosenthal, Beth, 1964- .
HV7436.G85 2007
363.330973—dc22   2006029404

Printed in the United States of America

Contents

Chapter 3: Can Gun Control Prevent School Violence?

Foreword

Indulging in a wide spectrum of ideas, beliefs, and perspectives is a critical cornerstone of democracy. After all, it is often debates over differences of opinion, such as whether to legalize abortion, how to treat prisoners, or when to enact the death penalty, that shape our society and drive it forward. Such diversity of thought is frequently regarded as the hallmark of a healthy and civilized culture. As the Reverend Clifford Schutjer of the First Congregational Church in Mansfield, Ohio, declared in a 2001 sermon, "Surrounding oneself with only like-minded people, restricting what we listen to or read only to what we find agreeable is irresponsible. Refusing to entertain doubts once we make up our minds is a subtle but deadly form of arrogance." With this advice in mind, Introducing Issues with Opposing Viewpoints books aim to open readers' minds to the critically divergent views that comprise our world's most important debates.

Introducing Issues with Opposing Viewpoints simplifies for students the enormous and often overwhelming mass of material now available via print and electronic media. Collected in every volume is an array of opinions that captures the essence of a particular controversy or topic. Introducing Issues with Opposing Viewpoints books embody the spirit of nineteenth-century journalist Charles A. Dana's axiom: "Fight for your opinions, but do not believe that they contain the whole truth, or the only truth." Absorbing such contrasting opinions teaches students to analyze the strength of an argument and compare it to its opposition. From this process readers can inform and strengthen their own opinions, or be exposed to new information that will change their minds. Introducing Issues with Opposing Viewpoints is a mosaic of different voices. The authors are statesmen, pundits, academics, journalists, corporations, and ordinary people who have felt compelled to share their experiences and ideas in a public forum. Their words have been collected from newspapers, journals, books, speeches, interviews, and the Internet, the fastest growing body of opinionated material in the world.

Introducing Issues with Opposing Viewpoints shares many of the well-known features of its critically acclaimed parent series, Opposing Viewpoints. The articles are presented in a pro/con format, allowing readers to absorb divergent perspectives side by side. Active reading questions preface each viewpoint, requiring the student to approach the material thoughtfully and carefully. Useful charts, graphs, and cartoons supplement each article. A thorough introduction provides readers with crucial background on an issue. An annotated bibliography points the reader toward articles, books, and Web sites that contain additional information on the topic. An appendix of organizations to contact contains a wide variety of charities, nonprofit organizations, political groups, and private enterprises that each hold a position on the issue at hand. Finally, a comprehensive index allows readers to locate content quickly and efficiently.

Introducing Issues with Opposing Viewpoints is also significantly different from Opposing Viewpoints. As the series title implies, its presentation will help introduce students to the concept of opposing viewpoints, and learn to use this material to aid in critical writing and debate. The series' four-color, accessible format makes the books attractive and inviting to readers of all levels. In addition, each viewpoint has been carefully edited to maximize a reader's understanding of the content. Short but thorough viewpoints capture the essence of an argument. A substantial, thought-provoking essay question placed at the end of each viewpoint asks the student to further investigate the issues raised in the viewpoint, compare and contrast two authors' arguments, or consider how one might go about forming an opinion on the topic at hand. Each viewpoint contains sidebars that include at-a-glance information and handy statistics. A Facts About section located in the back of the book further supplies students with relevant facts and figures.

Following in the tradition of the Opposing Viewpoints series, Greenhaven Press continues to provide readers with invaluable exposure to the controversial issues that shape our world. As John Stuart Mill once wrote: "The only way in which a human being can make some approach to knowing the whole of a subject is by hearing what can be said about it by persons of every variety of opinion and studying all modes in which it can be looked at by every character of mind. No wise man ever acquired his wisdom in any mode but this." It is to this principle that Introducing Issues with Opposing Viewpoints books are dedicated.

Introduction

"A well-regulated militia, being necessary to the security of a free state, the right of the people to keep and bear arms, shall not be infringed."

—The Second Amendment, U. S. Constitution

When the Bill of Rights, including the Second Amendment, was ratified in 1791, the United States was a very different place than it is today. The Revolutionary War had recently ended, giving the American colonies their independence from Britain. To fight that war, armed colonists had formed militias, which were state-sponsored emergency fighting forces. Each man was required to own a firearm and keep it in good condition so as to be ready to fight if needed. Militias were the preferred form of military organization because colonists were wary of having a standing, or permanent, army. It was thought that such an army could be used by a corrupt federal government to threaten the colonists' newly won freedoms. Though militias soon proved to be too expensive and cumbersome to maintain, the concern about possible government tyranny was reflected in the creation of the Second Amendment, granting the right to bear arms. Yet debate continues over exactly what the wording of the Second Amendment means and whether it is still relevant in contemporary society.

Gun rights advocates argue that the Second Amendment remains an important right for Americans. They believe the phrase "the right of the people to keep and bear arms" refers to an individual's right to own a gun for self-defense. After all, it is argued, an armed citizenry is critical for keeping government power in check and aggressive tyrants at bay. Writes analyst John R. Lott, "With more than a million people hacked to death with knives and cleavers over the last seven years, were the citizens of Rwanda and Sierra Leone better off without guns to defend themselves? What about the massacres of civilians in Bosnia? If Bosnians had possessed guns, would the massacres have taken place? And what about the Jews in the Warsaw ghetto during World War II?" These concerns do not only apply to citizens of other countries. Indeed, following Hurricane

At the Colorado state capitol, gun control advocates protest against the policies of the NRA, a staunchly pro-gun organization.

Katrina in September 2005, law enforcement officials in New Orleans ordered that all firearms be taken from citizens out of concern for emergency-worker safety. Gun rights advocates, however, saw this as an attempt to disarm citizens of their legal right to protect themselves—an especially critical ability considering the looting, violence, and chaos that followed Katrina. Because of opposition to this move, the Senate passed a bill in July 2006 barring the confiscation of legally owned guns during an emergency. Republican senator David Vitter of Louisiana was one of the bill's supporters. "Today's vote," he said, "sends a strong message that in the event of another disaster like Katrina, law-abiding Americans will be able to protect themselves without fear of government intruding upon their Second Amendment rights."

On the other hand, gun control advocates reject the claim that the Second Amendment guarantees each individual a right to bear arms.

They do not believe the Founding Fathers intended to grant private citizens the right to own guns for personal use. According to the Brady Center to Prevent Gun Violence, "Contrary to the gun lobby's propaganda, the Second Amendment guarantees the people the right to be armed *only in connection with service in a 'well regulated Militia.'* Courts consistently have ruled that there is no constitutional right to own a gun for private purposes unrelated to the organized state militia." For these reasons, gun control advocates argue that the right for private citizens to own guns is a misinterpretation of an antiquated law. Furthermore, gun control advocates argue, while guns are being purchased ostensibly to defend against the remote possibility of government abuse, they are doing great damage to American society. More than ten thousand murders are committed with guns every year, and terrifying trends, such as school shootings, are on the

Reflecting their belief in the Second Amendment right allowing citizens to bear arms, a group demonstrates in favor of gun ownership.

rise. Father Bruce Wellems, a Chicago pastor, has witnessed firsthand the damage guns can wreak on a neighborhood—his city had the country's highest murder rate in 2003. Says Wellems, "Many of the teachers, parents, social workers, counselors, and ministers in my neighborhood want to scream the same thing: 'Get the damn guns off the streets!'"

Gun ownership has a long history in the United States; so, too, does the continuing disagreement over how to interpret the Second Amendment. *Introducing Issues with Opposing Viewpoints: Gun Control* explores this and other debates about guns, including what measures might reduce gun violence and crime and whether or not school violence can be prevented by gun control. The articles presented highlight the widely divergent and strongly held beliefs of supporters of both gun control and gun ownership rights.

Chapter 1

Should People Have the Right to Own Guns?

Ownership and use of handguns has been a controversial issue for decades in the United States.

Handguns Should Be Banned

Kevin Fagan

"If none of us had had guns —most particularly, those handy little handguns —all these confrontations would have simply involved yelling, fists or perhaps knives."

In the following viewpoint, Kevin Fagan argues that handguns should be banned. Writing about his own personal experiences as a reporter with the *San Francisco Chronicle*, he warns that when faced with a split-second decision or in reaction to a stressful situation, many individuals will use a gun to solve a problem. While Fagan understands that a gun can save a life when used in self-defense, he contends that having a gun increases the chances of using it—even when it's not completely necessary. He maintains that banning guns will force people to solve problems without violence.

AS YOU READ, CONSIDER THE FOLLOWING QUESTIONS:

1. How does the author feel about using guns to hunt deer or to shoot at cans?
2. What personal experiences led Fagan to argue that guns should be banned?
3. According to the author, how many people die in England by handguns every year? In the United States?

My first real memory of a gun is from when I was 8, standing in a Nevada salt flat with my mother leaning over my right shoulder, folding my hand around the oh-so-smooth butt of a .22-caliber revolver. It was the gun she always kept under the car seat.

I squeezed off a shot at a rusty soda can 30 feet away, and the explosion in my ear and puff of sand alongside the can sent a shiver right to my toes.

"You'll get it, don't worry. You need to learn how to shoot this," my mother said, patting my head. "You never know how you might need it someday."

She was right. I did learn how to shoot, and I did need a gun someday . . . several somedays. And I came to respect the way a gun could save my life.

I also came to hate guns for the ways they have just as easily, just as coldly, unthinkingly, devastated life around me and come close to ending my own life time and again.

And I've come to believe guns have no logical, meaningful place in the lives of most ordinary people.

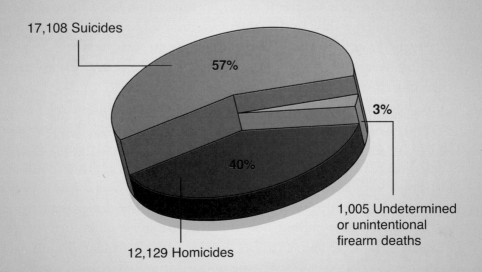

Deaths Caused by Firearms in the United States

17,108 Suicides

57%

3%

40%

1,005 Undetermined or unintentional firearm deaths

12,129 Homicides

Source: Deaths: Final Data for 2002. *National Vital Statistics Reports*; vol. 53, no. 5. Hyattsville, MD: National Center for Health Statistics, 2004.

There are plenty of Americans who have had the same relationship with this deadly little dealer of instant death. You could say the same thing about the country as a whole. It's a dysfunctional relationship, and there's not even a remotely easy way to fix it.

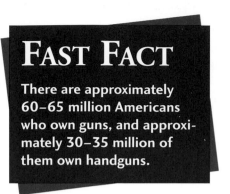

I'm not talking here about guns in the context of casual can-plinking, or deer hunting, both of which are plenty of fun (Bambi lovers, chill) and don't threaten anything if done right. I'm talking about the stuff that makes America the Wild West barbarian outpost which people from other countries shake their heads about. I mean the real gun stuff that happens when you're staring life in the face, not being chauffeured to Congress past the rabble so you can blather Second Amendment platitudes and cash your NRA [National Rifle Association] lobby checks.

Let me elaborate.

Guns Make It Too Easy to Kill

One relative of mine was blown away when he and his brother played stick-em-up, in the family barn; they didn't know the shotgun was loaded. Another was nearly blasted in half when a robber shot him through his front door. A cousin lost use of her arm for years after being shot in the Marin County Courthouse shootout of 1970; the judge's head was blown off as he sat next to her.

Those were the things I experienced, but didn't see. Other times guns cut closer.

In college in San Jose, I had to chase off attackers with a Luger 9mm semiautomatic when I lived alongside two warring gangs that promised to rub me out for telling the cops they shot holes in my windows and ripped off my car tires and gas. Years later, I had to replace that long-lost Luger with a .25-caliber semiautomatic when I was a young police reporter on a small-town newspaper and got a drug dealer mad at me.

I'd written a story about how this coke pusher kept squirming out of charges because the witnesses against him disappeared with each case. He told me to stop writing about him. When I gave him my

Journalism 101 lecture about the First Amendment and wrote again, he stomped into my newspaper office.

"You're dead, f—," he said, jamming his face close to mine. His rapsheet already included a juvenile sentence for murder and two assault convictions with knives and a shotgun. The local police commander shook his head when I asked what he could do to protect me. "Better get a gun, son," he said.

My dad's .25 was under my pillow the next night, after I'd spent the afternoon blasting at targets. At 2 a.m. someone came slamming on my door, and I sat in the living room with the gun pointed

Cagle Cartoons. Reproduced by permission of Cagle Cartoons, Inc. 2005

Should People Have the Right to Own Guns? 17

straight ahead, screaming, "Bring it on, f—!" at the door. Whoever was outside screamed back, "You're dead!" I yelled back again; this went on awhile, and then he went away.

No doubt: I would have fired. Just as I might have in other situations over the years when gangsters I was trying to interview stuck pistols in my guts or to my head, or when my wife was robbed at gunpoint in Berkeley.

And that's the trouble.

Find Other Ways to Solve Problems

If none of us had had guns—most particularly, those handy little handguns—all these confrontations would have simply involved yelling, fists or perhaps knives.

In Great Britain, about 50 people die by handguns every year. In America? It's about 9,000. I've lived in both places, and let me tell you, your radar for—and encounters with—danger are so drastically reduced across the water that they are nonexistent by comparison.

Absolutely, if you're a law-abiding citizen and some predator is pointing a barrel at you, you want a barrel of your own to end the argument. But as plain as the blood on the floor every day in America, that's a perpetual tit-for-tat that will always be awful.

The only way to fix this hideously dysfunctional relationship we in this country have with guns is to treat it like you would any other: End it before you wind up murdered. Nobody's saying this will be easy. The important things never are.

EVALUATING THE AUTHOR'S ARGUMENT:

In the viewpoint you just read, Kevin Fagan argues that allowing people to own guns could lead to unnecessary violence, particularly if the gun owners become emotionally upset or angry. He cites his own experiences as reasons for his belief. Were you convinced by Fagan's use of personal anecdotes? Why or why not?

Handguns Should Not Be Banned

Timothy Wheeler

"There are bad people in this world who will respond neither to reason nor to pleas, but only to force."

In the following viewpoint, Timothy Wheeler calls on the town of Wilmette, Illinois, to repeal its ban on gun ownership. He believes that banning guns prevents people from defending themselves. Wheeler argues that handgun bans are outdated and rely unfairly on the belief that anyone who owns a gun is a criminal or mentally ill. He maintains that the decreases in violent crime are due to longer jail sentences and stronger prosecution, and not to gun control.

Timothy Wheeler is the director of Doctors for Responsible Gun Ownership. He wrote this article for the *National Review*.

AS YOU READ, CONSIDER THE FOLLOWING QUESTIONS:

1. Why does the author feel that applying for a New York City gun permit is almost the same as a handgun ban?
2. According to Wheeler, why are laws banning handgun ownership based on prejudice?
3. What approaches have been responsible for the decrease in violent crime, in the opinion of the author?

T he good citizens of Wilmette, Ill., have a problem. Just before Christmas [2003] in this leafy, upscale Chicago suburb, homeowner Hale DeMar used his handgun to shoot a burglar. Trouble is, Wilmette years ago outlawed the ownership of handguns.

The career hoodlum who invaded DeMar's home was treated at a local hospital for a bad case of faulty-victim selection, and now awaits trial. Police are investigating whether he committed a string of robberies in the area.

Punishing the Wrong People

But instead of heaping honors on the brave homeowner who defended his family as any good father would do, the city of Wilmette has decided to prosecute him under the town's gun-ban ordinance. DeMar also faces the charge of failing to have a current firearm-owner's identification card.

DeMar's case is similar to that of another valiant home defender, this one in New York City. A burglar had broken into Ronald Dixon's house and was going through dresser drawers in his two-year-old son's room when Dixon shot him. New York City doesn't ban handguns outright, but the bureaucratic wall a prospective handgun owner must surmount is practically the same as a ban.

Dixon's handgun-permit application had not yet been approved, and he was forced to plead guilty to a lesser charge or face prosecution for gun possession. Had it not been for a nationwide public outcry he surely would have served serious prison time, rather than the three days he spent in jail. Apparently even those notoriously antigun-rights New York prosecutors don't want to appear anti-self-defense.

Banning Handguns Only Hurts Law-Abiding Citizens

Why would inhabitants of two large urban areas outlaw handguns, the best home-defense firearms? It can't be for tactical reasons. Shot-

Most handgun owners are law-abiding citizens. This woman trains in gun safety, exercising her right to bear arms.

guns and rifles are not as safe as handguns for densely populated city neighborhoods. These more powerful firearms are suitable for some self-defense scenarios, but they have a greater tendency than handguns to penetrate walls and cause unintentional injury or property damage.

No, in both cases the laws banning handgun ownership are rooted in prejudice. In New York that prejudice took the form of the Sullivan Law of 1911 [which required a police permit to own a gun], originally directed against southern-European immigrants. Wilmette's gun-ban ordinance was enacted in 1989 after a deranged woman shot several children in a local school. The townspeople apparently believe handguns are the tools of criminals or the mentally unbalanced, evil instruments that right-thinking people have no need for. It's a common misconception—one that is increasingly challenged in morality plays such as the Wilmette incident.

City folk seem to be slow learners on this one. But the rest of the country—the red states—long ago began rethinking their approach to violent crime. More violent felons than ever before are serving longer prison terms. Sentence enhancements, three-strikes laws, and vigorous prosecution of gun-wielding criminals have put many of the worst offenders out of business. That this should result in sharp decreases in violent crime should surprise no one. It's been well known for decades that most violent crimes are committed by a relatively small group of career criminals.

Allow People to Defend Themselves

At the same time, the public has awakened to the notion that the Hale DeMars and Ronald Dixons of the world are not the problem. There is something admirable about people with the courage to defend their homes. Some people in Wilmette are likely still squeamish about handguns. But even they cannot dispute the success of neighbor DeMar's intervention. Further evidence of public doubts about handgun bans is seen in the behavior of presidential candidates from the party of gun control—the Democrats. They are grabbing the nearest shotgun to pose for photo ops touting their newfound friendship with hunters and by extension, they hope, all gun owners.

The war on terrorism has reminded previously complacent Americans of some ancient truths about human nature, making them suspicious of the old nostrum of appeasement. There are bad people in this world who will respond neither to reason nor to pleas, but only to force. Even one such offender is toxic to a whole community, as many anxious Wilmette citizens can attest. But even one defender provides a powerful antidote, granting a protective effect that radiates well beyond his own home. Conversely, it hurts us all to punish a courageous neighbor who is willing to stand up to a tyrant like the burglar of Wilmette.

The people of Wilmette must now explain to us why they believe Hale DeMar was right in using lethal force to protect his family but wrong in using the only safe instrument for the job—a handgun. One way they could begin to atone for the persecution of this good man is to make a life-affirming New Year's resolution to repeal their handgun ban.

EVALUATING THE AUTHOR'S ARGUMENT:

In the viewpoint you just read, Timothy Wheeler believes that people should have the right to own guns and to use them to defend themselves and their families in their homes. Do you agree? Why or why not?

Viewpoint 3

People Should Have the Right to Carry a Concealed Weapon

Don B. Kates Jr.

"If you or your family are threatened by serious violence, the only real defense you have depends on you having a gun."

In the following viewpoint, Don B. Kates Jr. argues that the right to carry a concealed handgun is essential because police cannot defend all citizens against violence. Citing cases in which even restraining orders did not result in police protection, Kates maintains that people can only depend on themselves for protection.

Don B. Kates Jr., a civil-liberties lawyer and a former professor of constitutional law, wrote this article for *Handguns* magazine.

AS YOU READ, CONSIDER THE FOLLOWING QUESTIONS:

1. In the opinion of the author, under what circumstances can the police protect an individual directly?

2. Why does Kates feel that restraining orders are sometimes useless?

3. Why do some businesses forbid customers who are carrying a concealed weapon from entering their stores, according to the author?

Today the overwhelming majority of states have adopted laws under which law-abiding, responsible, qualified adult applicants are entitled to be issued permits to carry concealed handguns. But what about the advice given by innumerable anti-gun mayors and lobby groups that you do not need a gun because "the police are here to protect you?" Well, the anti-gun groups may be uninformed enough to believe this falsehood, but the mayors are not. Whenever

Jessica Gonzales believes police did not adequately protect her family when her husband shot and killed their three girls (shown in portrait).

cities are sued for failure to protect individuals, the mayors send forth their lawyers to invoke the "fundamental principle of American law that a government and its agents are under no general duty to provide public services, such as police protection, to any individual citizen." Though that quote happens to be from a District of Columbia court, the same rule is accepted in every state—see *Braswell v. Braswell*, 410 S.E.2d 897, 901 (N.C. 1991): "The general common-law rule, known as the public-duty doctrine, is that a municipality and its agents act for the benefit of the public, and therefore, there is no liability for the failure to furnish police protection to specific individuals."

The latest case to this effect is *Castle Rock, Colo., v. Gonzales*, decided by the U.S. Supreme Court on June 27, 2005. The facts alleged in the plaintiff's case against the city (which were assumed true by the court for purposes of its decision) were that her husband, Simon Gonzales, violated a restraining order by kidnapping his three daughters but that police did not go get him even though she told them where he was. Several hours later he went to a police station and committed "suicide by cop," getting into a shoot-out with officers. The little girls' bodies were later found in his car.

You Cannot Expect the Police to Protect You

In line with all the state cases I have mentioned, the Supreme Court ruled that individuals have no right to police protection under the federal Constitution. You see, you are the one who is legally required to defend yourself and your family—even if state law prohibits you having the means to do so. The police do not exist to protect individuals directly. They exist only to perform the general duties of (a) deterring crime by general patrol and (b) investigating after a crime has occurred to detect who committed it. The police simply do not have the resources to protect individuals threatened with criminal attack.

There are exceptions to this general doctrine; for instance, if the police explicitly promise a specific person, e.g. an informer, that they will protect him, then they have assumed a duty to him and may be liable. What the plaintiff was arguing in the *Gonzales* case was that her having a restraining order was an exception that entitled her to special protection. *Gonzales* was a 7-2 decision, and it bears emphasis that the two dissenters did not question the general rule. Their opinion started off by reiterating the rule that there is no right to police protection. Their argument was only that the restraining order should be deemed to make the situation an exception.

Restraining Orders Don't Work

The fact is that restraining orders are useless against anyone who is contemplating serious violence. If the penalties for kidnapping and murder do not deter someone, why would he be stopped by the minor penalty for violating a court order?

No, if you or your family are threatened by serious violence, the only real defense you have depends on you having a gun. This brings me back to the increasing number of states with laws that require that responsible, law-abiding, qualified adult applicants must be given permits to carry concealed handguns.

FAST FACT

According to the Citizens Committee for the Right to Keep and Bear Arms, more than 3 million Americans have permits allowing them to carry a concealed weapon.

The strength of the public support for these wise laws is illustrated by two recent developments in Minnesota. The following facts were given me by Hamline University law professor Joseph Olson, who heads the Gun Owners Civil Rights Alliance, which spearheaded the fight that resulted in passage of such a law, the Minnesota Citizen's Personal Protection Act of 2003.

Minnesota is a very liberal state, the home of such outstanding liberal leaders as Hubert Humphrey, Walter Mondale and Paul Wellstone. Under the old discretionary permit law, Minneapolis, St. Paul and many other cities exercised their discretion by denying carry licenses to all applicants except some persons with special influence. But the discretion to deny permits was virtually abolished by the 2003 Act.

However, on April 12, 2005, that Act was struck down by an anti-gun court on a legal technicality. The result was an overwhelming outcry by Minnesotans. Inundated by calls and emails from angry gun owners, one legislator promised that he would vote for a new bill that would correct the technicality and asked Prof. Olson to "turn it [the flood of angry constituents] off." Olson replied that the court decision had "turned it on" and that he had no power to turn it off; only passage of the new law could do that.

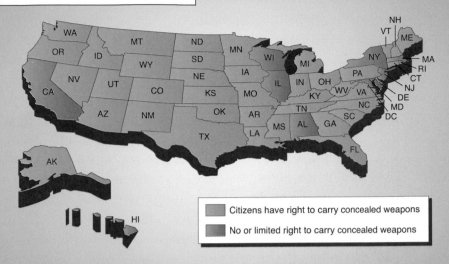

Right to Carry Laws 2006

Citizens have right to carry concealed weapons

No or limited right to carry concealed weapons

Source: National Rifle Association of America, Institute for Legislative Action, "Right to Carry Laws 2006," April 6, 2006. Reproduced by permission.

The new law resurrecting the Act went from introduction in the legislature to passage in the five weeks following the court decision. This appears to be a new record in Minnesota for how rapidly a law can be enacted.

Allow Citizens to Legally Carry Their Weapons

One aspect of the Minnesota legislation and the similar "shall issue" laws of many other states is that businesses may forbid customers or employees to carry a firearm in their store even though the customer has a CCW (carry concealed weapon) permit. In some states anti-gun activists have advised businesses to forbid gun carrying by customers or employees. This advice is also given by overcautious lawyers worried that a wrongful shooting by a CCW permittee might expose the business to liability.

Under the Minnesota legislation, the only way to bar CCW permittees from bringing their guns into the store is by the posting of a large sign on the store front. But the posting of signs banning CCW permittees from carrying their handguns on business premises sometimes generates big controversies. In the spring of 2004, a Home Depot store in Maple Grove, Minnesota, posted such a sign. It is not clear whether this was done on the initiative of the manager or as a matter of Home Depot policy. In any event, within hours a picture of the sign and adverse commentary about it were posted on the Internet by angry customers of the Maple Grove store. This prompted calls to Home Depot nationally and to local stores throughout the nation. Callers posted on the Internet that they had been told by Home Depot that the sign expressed its policy, which would shortly be in force in its stores nationwide.

The result was an alleged 1.8 million complaints to Home Depot, including one from a builder who claimed to spend upward of $1 million yearly at Home Depot and said he was now switching to a competing chain. In the space of less than 10 days Home Depot's position moved from the Maple Grove store's sign was consistent with its national policy, to the sign was unauthorized because Home Depot was simply considering the issues, to thanking customers for bringing the sign to Home Depot's attention because it was contrary to Home Deport policy and was being removed immediately, nor would any Home Depot store ever have such a policy.

EVALUATING THE AUTHOR'S ARGUMENT:

In this viewpoint, Don B. Kates Jr. discusses the controversy started when a Home Depot store in Maple Grove, Minnesota, banned customers from carrying concealed weapons into the store. What do you think—should people be allowed to carry concealed weapons into Home Depot and other stores? What is your opinion of the way Home Deport settled the controversy? Explain your answer thoroughly.

Viewpoint

4

People Should Not Have the Right to Carry a Concealed Weapon

"A conceal and carry law could potentially result in more loaded handguns in the environment."

Stephen W. Hargarten

In the following viewpoint, Stephen W. Hargarten, writing in the *Wisconsin Medical Journal*, warns about the possible effects of a law in Wisconsin that would permit the carrying of a concealed weapon. He argues that an increase in the number of handguns in society could lead to an increase in the suicide rate among children and teens. He is critical of the possibility that organizations would be able to apply for permits for individuals, which would make it difficult to identify who ultimately is obtaining the permit.

Stephen W. Hargarten is a medical doctor and the chair of the Emergency Medicine Department and codirector of the Firearm Injury Center, both of which are at the Medical College of Wisconsin.

Stephen W. Hargarten, " Public Health Implications of Carrying Concealed Weapons: Have We Thought This Policy Through?" *Wisconsin Medical Journal,* 2005, p. 19–20. Reproduced by permission.

AS YOU READ, CONSIDER THE FOLLOWING QUESTIONS:

1. In the author's opinion, why would young people be more affected than others by the conceal-and-carry legislation?

2. How many conceal-and-carry permit applications does Hargarten estimate will be made in the first year of the legislation? How many over five years?

3. According to the author, what percentage of police officers are killed with their own weapons while on duty?

The Wisconsin Legislature was one vote away [in 2004] from overriding Governor [Jim] Doyle's veto of legislation that would have allowed individuals to carry concealed weapons ("conceal and carry"). Because the override failed, at the time of this writing Wisconsin remains one of four states that prohibit the concealed carrying of dangerous weapons by civilians. Legislators who supported [2004]'s efforts have already indicated their intent to reintroduce such "personal protection" legislation and supportive organizations have promised a vigorous advocacy campaign to garner passage and enough votes to override another veto. [The bill failed again after the legislature upheld Gov. Doyle's veto a second time on Feb. 1, 2006.] During previous debate, the potential impact of conceal and carry laws on the public's health and on injury experience was not fully investigated or discussed. It is imperative that policy-makers and the public should vigorously discuss the implications of conceal and carry legislation from an evidence-based perspective of public health risk and benefit.

More Guns, More Deaths

The primary issue to be addressed is why this legislation is needed. The policy discussion about conceal and carry laws has been largely focused on crime, with supporters arguing that personal protection with firearms lowers the crime rate. A recent report of the National Academies of Science has concluded, however, that the available body of research does not support claims that conceal and carry laws have a measurable impact on crime. The recent rise in the number of homicides committed in Milwaukee suggests that policy-makers should focus on policies that have a known measurable effect and that these leaders examine multiple strategies that affect behavior, access to lethal means, and the environment.

A main concern about the conceal and carry legislation is the potential public health risk of injury to vulnerable populations, especially youth. Wisconsin's youth suicide rate is 36% higher than the national rate. A conceal and carry law could potentially result in more loaded handguns in the environment. We know that almost 60% of youth firearm suicides in Wisconsin involve someone else's gun; 83% of the time, it belongs to a parent or guardian. Are we really certain that conceal and carry is a thoughtful, timely policy for Wisconsin?

Defective Gun Worries

In the event of such legislation succeeding in this legislative session, two important issues should be considered. First, what kinds of

Wisconsin governor Jim Doyle speaks at a press conference in 2003, explaining why he vetoed legislation allowing the carrying of concealed weapons.

guns should be allowed to be concealed and carried? There is little information about the type and characteristics of firearms associated with deaths and injuries. Additionally, the safety of particular types of firearms should be studied. Design defects in firearms contribute to unintended fatalities. One such design defect, exposed

Avowing that he will carry a concealed weapon regardless of the law, a man shows how he conceals his handgun.

hammers that rest on firing pins, is present in the Ruger Blackhawk revolver, and has been associated with over 40 deaths and numerous injuries. Anecdotal accounts reflect the tragic outcomes that can occur when unsafe handguns are carried. For example, a Davis D-32 derringer with an exposed hammer resting directly on the firing pin was carried into a public setting, dropped, and discharged, injuring two women.

The design and safety characteristics of firearms should be taken into account when determining the types of weapons that may be carried concealed. This is particularly important since past legislation would have immunized firearm manufacturers and dealers from liability for design negligence. Unlike almost all other consumer products, there is no national product safety oversight of firearms. Legislators may wish to limit the availability of more dangerous firearms through safety standards such as California's "drop safety" requirement for all new handguns sold in the state. The standards applied by the federal government to the importation of handguns could also be adopted to assure standard safety features.

It is estimated that as many as 30,000 applications for permits will be made in the first year of conceal and carry and that as many as 100,000 permits will be issued over a 5-year period. The public health implication, of tens of thousands of individuals carrying handguns with a spectrum of potential safety defects have not been adequately discussed.

Emerging technologies, such as personalized handguns that would be inoperable to unauthorized users, should be critically examined. There has also been no evaluation of the risk that a legitimate conceal and carry permit holder could have his or her handgun forcibly taken away and used for criminal purposes. One study of law enforcement fatalities has found that 21% of officers killed with handguns while on duty were killed with their own service weapons.

Who Has the Permits?

Second, how are we going to know if this policy has had a positive or negative effect? The National Academies of Science report recommends that more comprehensive data and analysis are essential to the development and evaluation of policies and programs that involve firearms. Currently, states like Wisconsin are unable to fully evaluate the effects

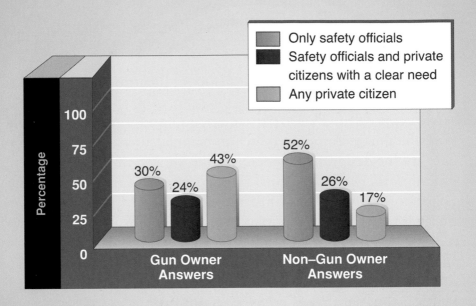

Who Should Be Allowed to Carry Concealed Weapons? Gun Owners vs. Nonowners

Legend:
- Only safety officials
- Safety officials and private citizens with a clear need
- Any private citizen

Gun Owner Answers
- 30%
- 24%
- 43%

Non–Gun Owner Answers
- 52%
- 26%
- 17%

Percentage axis: 0, 25, 50, 75, 100

Source: Who Should Be Allowed to Carry Concealed Weapons, Gun Owners vs. Non-Owners in "Public Wary About Broad Concealed Firearm Privileges," http://poll.gallup.com/content/default.aspx?ci+16822 (accessed Feb. 25, 2006). Copyright © 2005 by the Gallup Organization. Reproduced by permission of the Gallup Organization.

of conceal and carry legislation. Expanded support of Wisconsin's new Violent Death Reporting System (WVDRS) would contribute greatly to the state's capacity to evaluate these and other weapons-related policies. Provisions contained in Wisconsin's previous proposed conceal and carry legislation would have made the evaluation capacity difficult by impeding or prohibiting the use of license application information or the experience of license holders either as perpetrators or as victims of crime and violent injury. Such information will be necessary to assess the public health and criminal justice impact of conceal and carry legislation. A new concern arises as provisions are being drafted in this session's bill that would allow private firms or law enforcement groups to issue the conceal and carry permits and immunizing these groups from possible lawsuits. Decentralization of the licensing process creates further concern about data collection and adequate evaluation of the legislation.

Would This Help Reduce Crime?

Failure to address the public health implications of conceal and carry policies and practices may have unintended consequences for the health of the public. Do we really need this policy implemented to address crime and homicide? Do we want loaded, defective, or poorly-designed guns in our environment? Do we have the funds and infrastructure to accurately evaluate this policy?

Everyone needs to examine these issues critically before adopting a conceal and carry personal protection legislation. Physicians, public health professionals, criminal justice professionals, policy-makers, and the public should engage in a broader evidence-based public health policy discussion.

EVALUATING THE AUTHORS' ARGUMENTS:

In the viewpoint you just read, Stephen W. Hargarten argues against allowing people to carry concealed weapons because of concerns about the effects on society, including teen suicide and defective weapons. In the previous viewpoint, Don B. Kates Jr. contends that people should be permitted to carry a concealed weapon because the police are not able to protect each individual. In your opinion, which argument is more persuasive? Explain your reasoning.

Chapter 2

What Measures Will Reduce Gun Violence and Crime?

Security camera videotape shows Eric Harris (left) and Dylan Klebold heavily armed inside the Columbine High School cafeteria on April 20, 1999.

Gun Control Can Reduce Violence and Crime

Emanuel Margolis

"The proliferation of handguns on our streets . . . has resulted in the deaths and serious injuries of tens of thousands of Americans every year."

One response to the recent shootings in churches, schools, and courtrooms has been to pass legislation that will permit more people to carry guns for the purpose of self-defense. In the following viewpoint, Emanuel Margolis argues that making more guns available will result in more violence. Citing the rash of gun shootings in public places, he maintains that recent gun rights legislation has not helped reduce violence. Margolis contends that even background checks done prior to a gun sale are not taken seriously, arguing that thirty-five people were allowed to buy weapons even though their names were on a terrorist watch list. He declares that society must regulate itself to keep its citizens safe.

Emanuel Margolis practices law in Stamford, Connecticut. He wrote this article for the *Connecticut Law Tribune*.

AS YOU READ, CONSIDER THE FOLLOWING QUESTIONS:

1. How many firearm deaths were there in 2002, according to Margolis?
2. In the author's opinion, what does the Second Amendment guarantee?
3. According to Margolis, how many states now issue permits to carry a concealed weapon?

The headline read: "Shootings Fuel a Drive to Ease Gun Laws." After I had done a double-take, the full story in the *New York Times* of April 3rd [2005] bore out its accuracy.

Level the Playing Field?

A man in Wisconsin had opened fire in a church service, killing seven people and then himself. The district attorney offered a quick-fix solution. "The problems aren't the guns," he said, "it's the guns in the wrong hands. We need to put more guns in the hands of law-abiding citizens." The D.A., who recently announced his candidacy for Wisconsin attorney general, argued that the proliferation of guns would "level the playing field."

The horrifying shootings of [2005]—the family of a federal judge in Chicago, the deadly school killings in the Red Lake Indian Reservation, the shootings in courthouses in Atlanta and Tyler, Texas—appear to be fueling efforts to expand or pass legislation permitting concealed handguns. In Texas and Illinois, the shootings have spurred new legislation to allow judges and prosecutors to be armed. There have been proposals for arming teachers. In Nebraska and Wisconsin, legislators are feeling encouraged in their efforts to promote concealed weapons laws.

More Deaths from Guns

The proposals for cure are worse than the disease. Instead of antitoxins we are being offered protoxins. The proliferation of handguns on our streets, public buildings and homes has resulted in the deaths and serious injuries of tens of thousands of Americans every year, and the numbers keep rising. In 2002, the total number of deaths from firearms was 30,242, increasing by more than 1,500 over the total for 2000. Deaths from guns in 2002 were almost twice the number of alcohol-related traffic fatalities.

But isn't the right to protect oneself a fundamental one? Is there a more important human right than the right to self-defense, as codified in our criminal law? Isn't the right to bear arms enshrined in the Second Amendment to the Constitution, and part and parcel of the Bill of Rights?

There Is No Individual Right to Own a Gun

As early as May of 2001, then Attorney General John Ashcroft wrote a letter to the executive director of the National Rifle Association [NRA] stating "unequivocally my view" that the Second Amendment

Gun Control Laws Around The World

Country	Do gun owners need a license?	Do firearms need to be registered?	Other Restrictions	Households with firearms (%)	Gun Death Rate per 100,000
Japan	Yes	Yes	Prohibits handguns with few exceptions	0.6%	0.07
Singapore	Yes	Yes	Most handguns and rifles prohibited	0.01%	0.24
U.K.	Yes	Yes	Prohibits handguns	4.0%	0.4
Netherlands	Yes	Yes		1.9%	0.55
Spain	Yes	Yes	Some handguns and rifles are prohibited	13.1%	0.74
Germany	Yes	Yes		8.9%	1.44
Australia	Yes	Yes	Banned semiautomatics unless good reason	16.0%	2.94
Canada	Yes	Yes	Assault weapons and some handguns	26.0%	3.95
France	Yes	Yes, except sporting rifles		22.6%	5.48
Switzerland	Yes	Yes		27.2%	5.74
Finland	Yes	Yes		50.0%	6.65
USA	In some states	Handguns in some states	Some weapons in some states	41.0%	13.47

Source: Adapted from W. Cukier, "Firearms Regulation: Canada in the International Context," *Chronic Diseases in Canada*, April 1998 (statistics updated to reflect most recent figures, January 2001).

"clearly protect[s] the right of individuals to keep and bear firearms." This position was formally advocated by the Justice Department before the Supreme Court one year later in two of its briefs.

It will be recalled that the Second Amendment begins with the words "A well regulated Militia, being necessary to the security of a free State. . . . The prevailing Supreme Court doctrine, from at least as far back as its decision in *United States v. Miller* (1939), is that the Second Amendment provides for the collective right of self-defense, not a personal or individual right.

[Supreme Court] Justices Antonin Scalia's and Clarence Thomas's views to the contrary notwithstanding, as expressed in their dicta [opinions] in the gun control decision in *Printz v. United States* (1997), several federal circuit courts recently have held that the Second Amendment guarantees only a collective right to bear arms. These decisions, as well as the vast majority of scholarship in the field which support them, apparently were lost on Ashcroft in his zealous advo-

Cagle Cartoons, Reproduced by Permission of Cagle Cartoons, Inc.

cacy of the NRA position on guns, a government policy climaxed by the refusal of Congress to renew its ban on assault weapons [in 2004].

Despite Deaths, Guns Get the Green Light

Thirty-five states now authorize their weapons licensing agencies to issue permits to applicants for concealed handguns as long as they do not have criminal records; Alaska and Vermont allow concealed weapons without a permit. Despite the bloodletting directly resulting from shootings—even massive ones such as Columbine High School and the Red Lake Reservation—concealed weapons legislation is spreading. Within the past two years [2003–2005], five states, most recently Ohio, have passed concealed weapons laws.

With the passage of such handgun-friendly laws, the state legislatures have leapfrogged over the Second Amendment issue of collective versus individual right. In its last word on the subject (*Miller*), the Supreme Court held that the Second Amendment protects only those rights that have "some reasonable relationship to the preservation of efficiency of a well regulated militia."

Guns—and People—Need to Be Regulated

A recent Government Accountability Office examination of "background checks" for gun sales during a five-month period [in 2004] found 44 checks in which the buyer's name showed up on a government terrorist watch list; 35 of them were permitted to buy guns. Can it be that it is our own citizenry who need to be "well regulated" as being "necessary to the security of a free State?"

EVALUATING THE AUTHOR'S ARGUMENT:

In the viewpoint you just read, the author is wary of letting more people carry weapons for self-defense. He believes the availability of more guns will lead to more violence. Do you agree? What do you think might be the effect of more guns in public—less violence, or more? Explain your answer.

Gun Control Cannot Reduce Violence and Crime

Larry Elder

"A gun can be used to scare away an intruder without a shot being fired."

In the following selection Larry Elder argues that guns reduce violence and crime when used for self-defense. Drawing on studies about guns and crime, he maintains that when guns are used by victims, injury and death can be avoided. He criticizes the media for not publicizing instances in which people have used guns to protect themselves.

Larry Elder, an attorney and syndicated columnist, wrote this article for *Human Events*.

AS YOU READ, CONSIDER THE FOLLOWING QUESTIONS:

1. According to the author, what happens when a robbery victim fights back with a gun?
2. Why is having a gun in your home enough to scare off a robber, according to Elder?
3. According to criminologist Gary Kleck, how many lives are saved by guns every year?

Forty-six-year-old Joyce Cordoba stood behind the deli counter while working at a Wal-Mart in Albuquerque, New Mexico. Suddenly, her ex-husband—against whom Ms. Cordoba had a restraining order—showed up, jumped over the deli counter, and began stabbing Ms. Cordoba. Due Moore, a 72-year-old Wal-Mart customer, witnessed the violent attack. Moore, legally permitted to carry a concealed weapon, pulled out his gun, and shot and killed the ex-husband. Ms. Cordoba survived the brutal attack and is recovering from her wounds.

Using a Gun for Self-Defense Saves Lives

This raises a question. How often do Americans use guns for defensive purposes? We know that in 2003, 12,548 people died through non-suicide gun violence, including homicides, accidents and cases of undetermined intent.

UCLA professor emeritus James Q. Wilson, a respected expert on crime, police practices and guns, says, "We know from Census Bureau

Women from a pro-gun group practice shooting skills. Many women carry handguns for self-defense.

surveys that something beyond a hundred thousand uses of guns for self-defense occur every year. We know from smaller surveys of a commercial nature that the number may be as high as two-and-a-half or three million. We don't know what the right number is, but whatever the right number is, it's not a trivial number."

Criminologist and researcher Gary Kleck, using his own commissioned phone surveys and number extrapolation, estimates that 2.5 million Americans use guns for defensive purposes each year. He further found that of those who had used guns defensively, one in six believed someone would have been dead if they had not resorted to their defensive use of firearms. That corresponds to approximately 400,000 of Kleck's estimated 2.5 million defensive gun uses. Kleck points out that if only one-tenth of the people were right about saving a life, the number of people saved annually by guns would still be at least 40,000.

Guns Prevent Robberies and Injuries

The Department of Justice's own National Institute of Justice (NIJ) study titled "Guns in America: National Survey on Private Ownership and Use of Firearms," estimated that 1.5 million Americans use guns for defensive purposes every year. Although the government's figure estimated a million fewer people defensively using guns, the NIJ called their figure "directly comparable" to Kleck's, noting that "it is statistically plausible that the difference is due to sampling error." Furthermore, the NIJ reported that half of their respondents who said they used a gun defensively also admitted having done so multiple times a year—making the number of estimated uses of self-defense with a gun 4.7 million times annually.

Former assistant district attorney and firearms expert David Kopel writes, ". . . [W]hen a robbery victim does not defend himself, the robber succeeds 88 percent of the time, and the victim is injured 25 percent of the time. When a victim resists with a gun, the robbery success rate falls to 30 percent, and the victim injury rate falls to 17 percent. No other response to a robbery—from drawing a knife to shouting for help to fleeing—produces such low rates of victim injury and robbery success."

What do "gun control activists" say?

When the Threat of a Gun Is Enough
The Brady Center to Prevent Gun Violence's web site displays this oft-quoted "fact": "The risk of homicide in the home is three times greater in households with guns." Their web site fails to mention that Dr. Arthur Kellermann, the "expert" who came up with that figure, later backpedaled after others discredited his studies for failing to follow standard scientific procedures. According to *The Wall Street Journal*, Dr. Kellermann now concedes, "A gun can be used to scare away an intruder without a shot being fired," admitting that he failed to include such events in his original study. "Simply keeping a gun in the

A New Orleans shop owner issues a clear warning to any would-be looters in the aftermath of Hurricane Katrina in September 2005.

home," Kellermann says, "may deter some criminals who fear confronting an armed homeowner." He adds, "It is possible that reverse causation accounted for some of the association we observed between gun ownership and homicide—i.e., in a limited number of cases, people may have acquired a gun in response to a specific threat."

More Guns, Less Crime author John Lott points out that, in general, our mainstream media fails to inform the public about defensive uses of guns. "Hardly a day seems to go by," writes Lott, "without national news coverage of yet another shooting. Yet when was the last time you heard a story on the national evening news about a citizen saving a life with a gun? . . . An innocent person's murder is more newsworthy than when a victim brandishes a gun and an attacker runs away with no crime committed. . . . [B]ad events provide emotionally gripping pictures. Yet covering only the bad events creates the impression that guns only cost lives."

Guns Can Be Used for Protection

Americans, in part due to mainstream media's anti-gun bias, dramatically underestimate the defensive uses of guns. Some, after using a gun for self-defense, fear that the police may charge them for violating some law or ordinance about firearm possession and use. So many Americans simply do not tell the authorities.

A gunned-down bleeding guy creates news. A man who spared his family by brandishing a handgun, well, that's just water-cooler chat.

EVALUATING THE AUTHOR'S ARGUMENT:

The author of this viewpoint maintains that a robber can be chased away simply by being threatened with a gun. On the other hand, gun control advocates argue that a gun in a home is more likely to result in injury or death for someone living in the house. What do you think? Is it dangerous to keep a gun in a house, or is it a good precaution? Explain.

The Right to Shoot in Self-Defense Will Reduce Violence

"Victims shouldn't be punished for acting in self-defense against a serious threat."

Steve Chapman

In the following viewpoint, Steve Chapman argues that people should have the right to use a gun to defend themselves against the threat of serious injury or death. He discusses Florida's "stand your ground" law, which took effect on October 1, 2005. The law states that would-be victims do not need to try to escape before protecting themselves and will not be prosecuted for their actions. Chapman contends that the law is clear and reasonable and rightfully allows each person the chance for self-defense.

Steve Chapman is a writer whose articles have appeared in the *Chicago Tribune*, from which this viewpoint was taken.

AS YOU READ, CONSIDER THE FOLLOWING QUESTIONS:

1. According to Chapman, what happened to Florida's murder rate after it passed a law allowing people to carry concealed weapons?

2. Why should people be allowed to shoot an attacker instead of trying to escape, in Chapman's view?

3. What does the word *anathema* mean in the context of the viewpoint?

When Florida passed a law in 1987 making it easier for citizens to get licenses to carry concealed firearms, opponents predicted that blood would run in the streets. "When you have 10 times as many people carrying guns as you do now, and they get into an argument and tempers flash, you're going to have people taking out guns and killing people," one gun-control activist said.

Since the law was passed, it turns out, Florida's murder rate has been cut in half. Instead of becoming more dangerous, the state has become considerably safer.

With rare exceptions, the people carrying guns have done so responsibly. In the last 18 years, the state has granted more than 1 million conceal-carry permits. Only 155 people have had their licenses revoked for crimes involving firearms—one for every 7,000 licenses issued.

The warnings of gun-control advocates about that law were way off the mark. So when you hear them warn that another law concerning firearms will lead to unnecessary bloodshed in Florida, skepticism is in order.

The Legal Right to Protect Yourself

[In 2005], the Florida legislature passed a measure giving citizens more legal protection when they act in self-defense. That alarmed the Brady Campaign to Prevent Gun Violence, which describes the policy as "shoot first, ask questions never." Recently, the group handed out leaflets at the Miami airport to advise arriving passengers to exercise extreme caution: "Do not argue unnecessarily with local people. If someone appears to be angry with you . . . do not shout or make threatening gestures."

The new law gives greater protection to citizens who feel compelled to use deadly force when they are attacked in a public place. Before, someone facing "imminent death or great bodily harm" had an obligation to retreat if possible. Under the new rule, as David

After passage of Florida's "stand your ground" law, members of the Brady Campaign to Prevent Gun Violence hand out advisory flyers at the Miami airport.

Kopel of the Colorado-based Independence Institute puts it, "If a gang tries to mug you while you are walking down a dark street, and you draw a gun and shoot one of the gangsters, a prosecutor cannot argue that you should have tried to run away."

Opponents have characterized the change to mean any Floridian with a firearm can blast away with impunity. "I can picture a stressed-out Tampa soccer mom drawing a bead on an approaching panhandler and shrieking, 'Go ahead, make my day!'" fantasized *Time* magazine columnist Michelle Cottle.

Deadly Force Can Only Be Used for the Right Reasons

But the law doesn't say you can shoot anyone who approaches you on the street, or anyone who annoys you. It says you may resort to deadly force only if (1) you are attacked or threatened with violence and (2) you have good reason to fear being killed or badly hurt.

If a panhandler asks you for spare change, or even curses you, that wouldn't qualify. If a beefy, hostile biker screams that he's going to stomp you, or rape you, that probably would.

While the "stand your ground" rule may be new in the Sunshine State, it's old hat elsewhere. "The majority of American states have always held that a person who is attacked anywhere in a manner that threatens death or great bodily harm is entitled to use deadly force to resist, rather than retreating from the attacker," says criminologist Don Kates, author of several books on gun issues. But you don't see Brady Campaign staffers handling out fliers in the other states.

At a rally supporting the carrying of concealed weapons in Ohio, women display their handguns in plain sight, as required by law.

Trying to Escape Can Pose a Greater Danger

Why shouldn't people who are attacked have to look for an escape route before fighting back? One reason is that a victim may expose herself to additional risk by trying to flee from a criminal who is larger and faster than she is.

Another problem with the old rule is that if she makes the wrong decision and defends herself when she might arguably have gotten away, she can end up in prison. She can also be sued. Judging whether it's safe to flee is a split-second, life-and-death decision, and the penalty for being wrong—at least in the eyes of the police—can be heavy.

Supporters of the law think victims shouldn't be punished for acting in self-defense against a serious threat. The change reflects the view that it would not be a bad thing for criminals to face greater risks when they resort to violence. And it embraces the proposition—anathema to gun-control advocates—that self-defense is the fundamental right of every person.

It may be that the new law errs on the side of giving too much protection to victims of violent crime. But that beats erring on the side of giving them too little.

EVALUATING THE AUTHOR'S ARGUMENT:

In this viewpoint, Steve Chapman argues in favor of laws that allow people to shoot in self-defense. Michelle Cottle, author of the next viewpoint, disagrees. After reading both viewpoints carefully, which author do you side with? Why? Use points from the text to explain your answer.

Viewpoint 4

The Right to Shoot in Self-Defense Will Not Reduce Violence

Michelle Cottle

"Lethal force should be avoided whenever a reasonable alternative, like running away, is safely possible."

In the following viewpoint, Michelle Cottle opposes laws that allow individuals who feel threatened by another person to shoot them. She warns that such laws could lead to more violent confrontations. Furthermore, she argues it is wrong to encourage people to use violence rather than avoid it by escaping or deescalating a situation. Cottle believes that supporters of gun rights are taking the idea of protecting one's home too far by expanding it to include any public place.

Michelle Cottle is a senior editor at the *New Republic.* Her articles have appeared in the *New York Times*, the *Atlantic*, and *Time* magazine, from which this viewpoint was taken.

AS YOU READ, CONSIDER THE FOLLOWING QUESTIONS:

1. What does the quip offered by the author's father mean? Do you think it is true?

2. According to Cottle, what is the "Castle Doctrine"?
3. What did supporters of gun rights expand the meaning of *castle* to mean in this law, in the opinion of the author?

Despite my liberal credentials as a Volvo-driving, pro-choice, gay-marriage-supporting urban dweller, I admit to an inner conflict when it comes to guns. I grew up surrounded by firearms and the boys who loved them. My father is a bona fide hunting nut who threatened to buy my son a lifetime membership to the National Rifle Association [NRA] for his first birthday. I myself have mowed down a variety of defenseless woodland creatures. I used to be a decent shot with a pistol, and once during the Clinton years, I spearheaded an outing of lefty political scribes for a round of skeet shooting.

But while I appreciate guns, I also appreciate the need for gun laws. Without them, Dad's quip—"A well-armed society is a polite

caglecartoons.com

Jeff Parker © 2005 *Florida Today*. Reproduced by permission.

society"—holds true only if your idea of "polite" is something akin to HBO's *Deadwood* or the Sunni triangle. Which is why I'm perturbed by the Florida legislature's decision to pass a bill, signed into law by Governor Jeb Bush [April 26, 2005], allowing virtually anyone who feels threatened at any time and in any place to whip out a gun and open fire. The law decrees that a person under attack "has no duty to retreat and has the right to stand his or her ground and meet force with force, including deadly force if he or she reasonably believes it is necessary to do so to prevent death or great bodily harm to himself or herself or another or to prevent the commission of a forcible felony."

The Law Makes It Too Easy to Reach for Your Gun

"Stand his or her ground"? "Meet force with force"? Wow. It's as if the text of a real bill somehow got transposed with dialogue from a 1970s Dirty Harry paean to vigilantism. I can picture a stressed-out Tampa soccer mom drawing a bead on an approaching panhandler and shrieking, "Go ahead, make my day!"

Gun-control advocates are distraught over this development, predicting a rise in everything from road-rage episodes to gang violence. Gun toters may wrongly assume they have "total immunity from prosecution," said Miami police chief John Timoney. The law's supporters dismiss such concerns as liberal hysteria and extol the bill's passage as a victory for law-abiding citizens. Wayne LaPierre, the N.R.A.'s excruciating macho executive vice president, crowed, "[This will] make criminals pause before they commit their next rape, robbery or murder."

Taking the "Castle Doctrine" Too Far

I don't buy it, Wayne. The Florida courts, like those elsewhere, have long acknowledged that shooting someone in self-defense is, on occasion, a tragic necessity. It's just that, until now, most states have held to the notion that lethal force should be avoided whenever a reasonable alternative, like running away, is safely possible. The recognized exception is when a person's home has been invaded, at which point the home-owner may shoot first and ask questions later—a provision commonly referred to as the "Castle Doctrine." But the N.R.A. and Florida lawmakers apparently felt the definition of one's "castle"

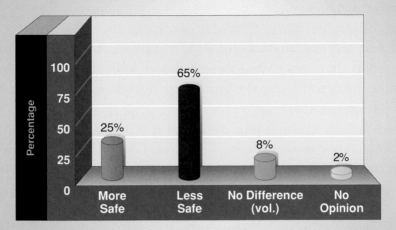

Americans Would Not Feel Safe Around Concealed Weapons

A 2005 Gallup poll found that nearly two in three Americans would feel less safe if they were in a public place and knew that concealed firearms were allowed. Twenty-five percent say it would make them feel safer, and 8 percent said that it would not make any difference to them.

Source: Feel More or Less Safe in Place Allowing Concealed Weapons? in "Public Wary About Broad Concealed Firearm Privileges," June 14, 2005, http://poll.gallup.com/default.aspx?ci=16822&pg=1&VERSION=p. Copyright © 2005 by the Gallup Organization. Reproduced by permission of the Gallup Organization.

needed broadening to include pretty much anywhere a person might happen to wander. Some drunk spoiling for a fight at your favorite bar? Don't "retreat" to another barstool. Flash the .44 Magnum in your shoulder holster and ask the punk if he feels lucky.

Unfortunately, this legislative absurdity is a problem for more than just Florida. A triumphant N.R.A. has vowed to get "stand your ground" laws passed in every state. "We will start with red and move to blue," LaPierre has declared, adding ominously, "Politicians are putting their career in jeopardy if they oppose this type of bill."

N.R.A. Believes Guns Can Solve All Problems

Though irritating, LaPierre's cockiness is perhaps justified. The Bush years have been good to the N.R.A. With Republicans running Washington, cowed Democrats are afraid to utter the words *gun control* even in the privacy of their homes. As a result, despite polls showing that most Americans support sensible gun laws, the N.R.A. has opposed even popular measures like renewing the 1994 ban on assault weapons (which Congress let lapse [in 2004]). At this point, the N.R.A. won't even support banning the sale of guns to terrorist suspects on the no-fly list. Pressed on the matter, LaPierre has piously asserted, "This is a list that somebody has just put a name on. These people haven't been indicted for anything. They haven't been convicted of anything."

Alas, despite its oft professed commitment to keeping weapons away from the bad guys, the N.R.A. clearly has no use for any gun laws—other than some Wild West, kill-or-be-killed law of the streets. But, hey, if that's the way the gun lobby thinks we should start handling disputes in this country, maybe it's time the Democratic Party stopped agonizing about gun control and started brushing up on its aim—if only for purposes of self-defense. I'd be happy to organize a trip to the skeet range anytime, guys. My Volvo seats five.

EVALUATING THE AUTHOR'S ARGUMENTS:

Michelle Cottle opens her viewpoint by writing about her appreciation for and experience with guns. Why do you think she chose this type of opening for an essay that could be considered anti-gun?

"Smart Guns" Can Reduce Violence and Crime

Ronald Brownstein

"[Let's] spur gun manufacturers to . . . prevent young people from killing with guns that don't belong to them."

In the following viewpoint, Ronald Brownstein argues that "smart gun" technology will lower violence and crime by reducing the number of stolen guns that can be used. The smart gun, which is currently in development, will be computerized with personalized sensors that would prevent anyone except the owner of the gun from using it. Because most school shooters steal their guns from adults, Brownstein argues that this technology could drastically reduce school massacres. Brownstein concludes the government should pursue this technology—and persuade gun manufacturers to help.

Ronald Brownstein is a columnist for the *Los Angeles Times*, from which this viewpoint was taken.

AS YOU READ, CONSIDER THE FOLLOWING QUESTIONS:

1. How many people did Jeff Weise kill at Red Lake High School, as reported by the author?

Ronald Brownstein, "A Smarter Way to Control Outbreaks of School Gun Violence," *Los Angeles Times*, March 28, 2005, p. A10. Copyright © Los Angeles Times. Reproduced by permission.

2. How does Brownstein define "dynamic grip recognition" technology?
3. In the opinion of the author, why did Smith & Wesson withdraw from an agreement to build smart guns and install gun locks?

I t's still true, as [Russian novelist] Leo Tolstoy wrote long ago, that every unhappy family is unique in its misery. But in our time, the bridge between private despair and public tragedy, especially for young people, is often the same: stolen guns.

So it was in the [March 21, 2005,] school massacre in Red Lake, Minn. No one can definitively say what created Jeff Weise's desire to kill. It may have had its roots in a shattered family, or an adverse re-action to antidepressant drugs, or simply humanity's innate capacity for evil.

Keeping Guns Out of the Hands of Children

But there's less mystery about the factor that created his ability to kill 10 people, including himself: When Weise shot his grandfather, a police sergeant, with a .22-caliber handgun and stole his shotgun and revolver, the young man's rage became much more dangerous to those around him.

In that way, the 16-year-old was hardly unique. Experts say that young people who commit school shootings often use guns stolen from adults; it could hardly be oth-erwise.

That pattern has drawn almost no attention in the killings' after-math. The White House, the politi-cal establishment and even the media have treated the Minnesota shooting spree—when they diverted their attention . . . long enough to notice it at all—as an inexplicable tragedy that underscored the per-sistence of school violence. But it ought to inspire us to ask what we

can do to make such tragedies less frequent and, when they occur, less deadly.

The answer has many pieces, from improvements in school security to more effective counseling for troubled youths. But part of it could be no more complicated than making it tougher for young people to use guns that don't belong to them. In an era of personalized technology, it seems reasonable to ask why it isn't possible to design guns that can't be fired by anyone except their authorized user.

Only Its Owner Could Fire the Gun

That's the question being explored by researchers at the New Jersey Institute of Technology in Newark. In 2002, the New Jersey Legislature passed a groundbreaking measure encouraging the development of so-called smart guns that would not fire for anyone except their authorized owner.

No such guns exist today. But the New Jersey statute said the state would permit the sale of only smart guns three years after any manufacturer brought to the market a viable model.

The New Jersey Institute of Technology has been working to develop such a firearm since 1999, the last few years with the help of federal funds secured by its two Democratic senators, Jon Corzine and Frank R. Lautenberg. The institute, part of the state university system, spent the first few years examining alternative approaches for personalizing a gun to prevent anyone but its owner from firing it.

For the last several years, the institute has focused on "dynamic grip recognition" technology. That's a system enabling sensors in a gun's handle to recognize the owner's grip and then block anyone else from firing it.

This firearm designed by the New Jersey Institute of Technology is a prototype of a "smart gun" with grip-recognition sensors.

"The basic concept is this—the way you grab the gun during the first incidence of the trigger pull becomes a coordinated and reflexive act," said Donald H. Sebastian, the institute's vice president for research and technology. "The fingerprint equivalent is the pressure pattern of your hand on the grip of the gun over time. We can see enough uniqueness in roughly the first tenth of a second of the trigger pull in order to be able to identify you as you."

The Technology Can Work

The research has progressed enough that the institute demonstrated a prototype at a shooting range in Bayonne, N.J., in December [2004]. But Sebastian estimates the effort is three years away from producing an actual gun that consumers will consider reliable enough to purchase.

The technical challenges are formidable.

Before it could be sold, the institute's smart gun would need to demonstrate that it could recognize its owner if he was wearing gloves, or grabbed the gun in an unusual way under stress, or even picked it up with the hand other than the one he normally uses. Since many people buy guns for personal protection, the margin for error is understandably low.

Yet Sebastian is confident, based on the research so far, that these technical problems can be overcome. And, indeed, smart guns fit with the steady development of technology personalizing products for their users.

"When the public becomes more familiar with personalization technology, such as computers, it will come to understand that the technology is feasible and ought to be applied to guns as well," said Stephen Teret, a professor at the Johns Hopkins Bloomberg School of Public Health in Baltimore.

Make Gun Manufacturers Help

Washington could accelerate that process if it focused more on the potential. After the shootings at Colorado's Columbine High School in 1999, President Clinton negotiated an agreement with Smith & Wesson in which the venerable gun maker agreed to develop smart guns, as well as to take other positive steps, such as installing locks on all guns.

But the company was battered by a boycott organized by gun-owner groups, which considered the deal a sellout of gun rights. After a change of ownership, Smith & Wesson cooled on the agreement, and President Bush allowed the company to back out of it. Today, that once-promising effort is a dead letter.

One of a president's greatest tools is the power to enlarge—or diminish—the parameters of the possible. Bush said nothing in public about the Minnesota shootings for days, and when he finally mentioned it, in his radio address [the following] Saturday, he alluded only to the need for more character education.

That's a worthwhile initiative. But the country deserves a more comprehensive approach to discouraging youth violence. Part of the answer could be expanded federal efforts to support the work in New Jersey and to spur gun manufacturers to explore other possibilities to prevent young people from killing with guns that don't belong to them. That's not left or right. It's just smart.

EVALUATING THE AUTHOR'S ARGUMENT:

In this viewpoint, Ronald Brownstein maintains that smart guns would help prevent school shootings because students would be unable to use someone else's gun. What are some advantages of this technology? What are some drawbacks? After carefully considering the matter, explain your opinion of how helpful smart guns may be in reducing school shootings.

"Smart Guns" Cannot Reduce Violence and Crime

Ralph D. Sherman

"Smart adults— a much more sensible solution than 'smart guns.'"

In the following viewpoint, Ralph D. Sherman argues that computerized, or "smart," guns cannot reduce violence and crime. He maintains there are too many problems with smart gun technology to make it practical, such as whether the sensors would be able to recognize the fingerprints of a gun owner wearing gloves. Sherman believes that smart guns cannot replace what is ultimately the responsibility of adults: to store their guns properly and to teach children about gun safety. Ralph D. Sherman is an attorney in Connecticut. He wrote this article for the Gunsafe Web site.

AS YOU READ, CONSIDER THE FOLLOWING QUESTIONS:

1. In the opinion of the author, why would a computerized gun not be safe in the hands of a criminal?

2. How many police officers are killed with their own weapons each year, according to Sherman?

3. What does the Eagle Eddie safety program teach children to do if they find a gun?

Ralph D. Sherman, "Children, 'Smart Guns,' and Smart Adults," www.gunsafe.org, Febuary, 2006. Reproduced by permission of the author.

Anyone who has watched science fiction movies in the past 20 years has seen a "smart gun"—a computerized gun that will fire only by an authorized user. In real life, however, such guns do not exist—and for good reasons.

There are two basic problems with a computerized gun. The first problem is that the gun may not fire when it should. The second problem is that the gun may fire when it shouldn't. Both situations are frightening. Both have caused legitimate manufacturers to back away from the concept.

"Smart" Guns Cause More Problems

Let's look at the first basic problem. If something goes wrong with the computer inside the gun, the gun may fail to fire when it's really needed. Computers are not foolproof, as anyone who uses an ATM or a word processor is aware. And a computer inside a gun would be subjected to tremendous physical force every time the gun is discharged. Think about taking a hammer to a laptop.

A gun that fails to fire when needed is not desirable to anyone who owns a firearm for self-defense. Although some police bureaucrats have advocated the computerized gun, no patrol officer wants such a gun in his or her duty holster. In actual tests computerized guns have never proven adequately reliable.

But even if the computer problem were solved, another real-life difficulty has prevented the production of guns that recognize authorized users. A gun that contains sensors to recognize fingerprints will not work when the user is wearing gloves. That means that police, hunters, or anyone who needs to use this type of gun outdoors in cold weather will have a problem.

A Computer Cannot Replace Proper Gun Storage

Those who advocate computerized guns say they would be safer because they can't be fired by children or by criminals. But does that mean that one could leave a computerized gun where a child could find it? Of course not. So child safety . . . would not really be improved by putting a computer inside the gun. The gun still must be stored so that children don't have access.

This brings us to the second basic problem. A computerized gun may fire when it shouldn't. But the computer "safety" feature will

It is doubtful that this computer microchip technology with scanning devices would prevent anyone but an authorized user from firing a gun.

nevertheless tempt some persons to store the gun where children can find it. (A study in the 1990s showed that "child-proof" aspirin containers actually caused the number of child poisonings to increase, because too many adults depend on the "child-proof" feature, instead of storing aspirin out of children's reach and teaching their children that aspirin is not candy.)

Another possible benefit of computerized guns is that they might be safe if they fall into the hands of criminals. That's the theory behind steering-wheel locks, too, but millions of cars are stolen every year. The fact is, if a criminal steals a gun, he'll have plenty of time, after he gets home, to open the gun and disable the safety mechanism. In fact, it may be very easy to do this.

For several years Colt's worked on a computerized gun, which never got past a prototype. At one point the big question was, what if the battery dies? Should the gun be designed so it fires or so it stays locked?

A Computerized Gun Could Still Be Used by a Criminal

Colt's had received a government grant to design the computerized gun for use by police. If a police officer were using the gun to defend himself, he'd want the gun to work even with a dead battery. So that's how the gun was designed. That means that if a criminal stole such a gun, all he would have to do is remove the battery. Then the gun would shoot for anyone.

Ironically, the original reason that computerized guns were proposed was that they might prevent police officers being murdered with their own guns. Somebody suggested that police officers were often disarmed by criminals and then murdered with their own guns. But the facts show that this is an extremely rare occurrence. Accord-

A technician holds up a "smart gun" and chip prototype. Critics say criminals could disable and then use a computerized gun.

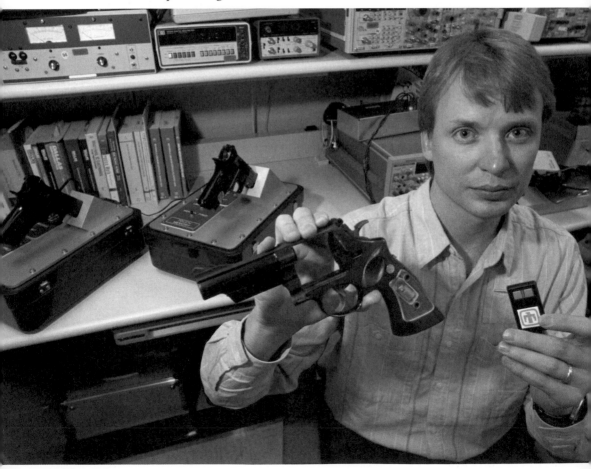

ing to the FBI, in a recent year six officers in the United States were killed with their own weapon. Every one of those cases is a tragedy, but that's six officers per year out of about 700,000 sworn officers in the entire United States—hardly a widespread occurrence.

In the late 1990s several gun manufacturers posted information on their web sites about their ongoing attempts to develop computerized guns. Today the web pages are gone. A firm in Oxford, Connecticut, that made a news splash with advanced fingerprint technology for guns has also disappeared. The company's web site promised that the technology would provide "a high degree of certainty" in the operation of computerized guns. The web site is gone.

It Is the Adult's Responsibility

A gun that operates with "a high degree of certainty" is at best unnecessary and at worst downright dangerous. Smart adults who have guns at home treat them as if they are always loaded, all the time. And smart adults treat children as if they are always curious, all the time. Smart adults teach children from an early age that guns are dangerous for children—the same as power saws, kitchen knives, and electrical outlets. Smart adults store guns in locked cabinets so that the guns are not accessible to children.

Smart adults also use the National Rifle Association's Eddie Eagle safety program, which teaches children what do to if they come across a gun when they are playing outside or at another home: Stop; don't touch; leave the area; tell an adult.

Smart adults—a much more sensible solution than "smart guns."

EVALUATING THE AUTHOR'S ARGUMENT:

In the viewpoint you just read, the author argues that adults teaching children about gun safety is a more effective approach to gun safety than developing "smart guns." Do you agree or disagree? Explain your answer using evidence from the text.

Chapter 3

Can Gun Control Prevent School Violence?

The day after the deadly shooting at Columbine High School in April 1999, students grieve for their classmates.

Gun Control Can Prevent School Shootings

Bruce Wellems

"When children kill children, we adults must do what we can to get the guns out of their hands."

In the following viewpoint, Bruce Wellems laments that America's youth has easy access to guns. This access, he argues, leads to the death of children in schools and on the streets. Introducing strict gun control could prevent school and street shootings, according to Wellems. He also believes that children should not be allowed to play violent video games or watch violent movies, arguing that society must teach children to value life so they respect themselves and others.

Wellems is the pastor of Holy Cross/Immaculate Heart of Mary Parish in Chicago. He wrote this viewpoint for *U.S. Catholic* magazine.

AS YOU READ, CONSIDER THE FOLLOWING QUESTIONS:

1. Which city had the highest murder rate in the country in 2003, according to the author?
2. Why does Wellems believe that many children enjoy firing guns?
3. Who is to blame for gun violence, in the opinion of the author?

There are times I can barely keep from screaming. And I'm not alone. Many of the teachers, parents, social workers, counselors, and ministers in my neighborhood want to scream the same thing: "Get the damn guns off the streets!"

My city has come in No. 1: Chicago had the most murders in the country [in 2003]. Even though the number dropped, it was still higher than that of New York or Los Angeles. Most of those murders, police tell us, are gang-related, and many were committed by young people—children, really. You can't have guns in the hands of children—even if they are 5 feet, 10 inches tall and look like adults.

It Is Too Easy for Children to Obtain Guns

In my neighborhood—which [in 2003] reported 31 homicides, the second highest number in the city—70 percent of the population is under the age of 18. According to the 2000 U.S. Census, an average of 150 children live on each of our blocks. Nobody yet has counted the guns per block, but I do know that any of those 150 children can purchase a gun just as easily as a video game.

So many afternoons we've had adults and children bring guns and ammunition to the rectory: "Can you please give these to the police?"

If you are a mom, what do you do? Does a time-out work when you catch your 13-year-old son hiding a gun in the house—the same house where your other five children live? What do you do when that same 13-year-old has already been arrested three times for gun possession? You don't find discipline tips on these situations in parenting books.

"Do you have a gun?" I asked one 15-year-old in my parish.

"Of course I do, Father. I have to defend my people. I have to keep them safe."

"Have you ever fired it?" I asked.

> **FAST FACT**
>
> Sixty-eight percent of student-attackers got their firearms from their own home or from the home of a relative, according to *The Final Report and Findings of the Safe School Initiative: Implications for the Prevention of School Attacks in the United States* by the U.S. Secret Service and U.S. Department of Education, May 2002.

Guns Cause the Most School-Related Violent Deaths

Total School-Related Deaths, 2004–2005: 39

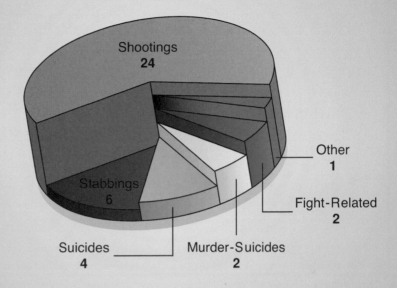

Shootings
24

Other
1

Stabbings
6

Fight-Related
2

Suicides
4

Murder-Suicides
2

Source: "Identified School-Related Violent Deaths: 2004-2005 School Year," *School Deaths, School Shootings, and High-Profile Incidents of School Violence.* Copyright © 2006 by National School Safety and Security Services. Reproduced by permission.

"Of course I have Father. I am a soldier and this is a war. I have to defend my family."

Finally I asked him, "Did you ever hit anyone?"

"Geez, Father, I don't know. I didn't open my eyes." He is still a young boy, afraid.

These children are drawn to guns. Many tell me that firing a gun makes them feel powerful and gives them an adrenaline rush. That's an irresistible combination for teens.

Let's Take the Guns Away from Kids

The gun lobby keeps telling us, "Guns don't kill people. People do." But I have a more accurate sound byte: "Our children kill children if they have guns."

Who's to blame? We can't focus the blame on just one group—the court system, the police, the legislators, the parents, the church, the media, or the gun lobby. Everybody shares the blame. But why even

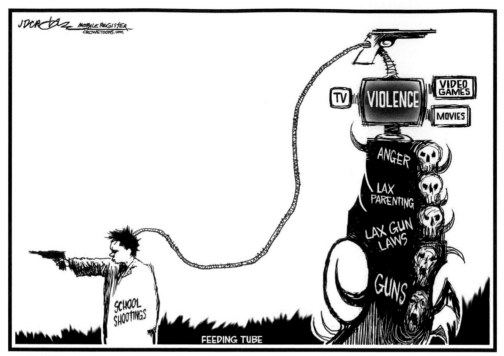

Mobile Register/crowetoons,com

waste energy blaming one another when we are burying our children and too many of our neighborhoods have makeshift memorials on their corners? Let's focus instead on how everybody is responsible for doing something.

Let's get rid of the guns. And let's ask people to help us.

In a neighborhood like ours it is difficult to collect guns. Sometimes I imagine just flying a helicopter over the whole neighborhood with a giant magnet attached. I will keep urging people to turn any gun they find into the rectory.

Our city's mayor, Richard M. Daley, will continue to hold the people who make the guns accountable for what happens after they are sold. Our legislators need to pass strong laws that outlaw assault weapons as well as give our children education and opportunities so they will walk away from guns and toward a better future.

It Is Society's Responsibility

Parents need to teach their children that it is not OK to be violent in their play, that it is not OK to play video games in which people are ripped apart or to watch movies in which the body count is higher than the director's IQ. We must help our parents learn how to parent without violence, how to talk to their children, how to respect and, above all, love their children.

If we look to Jesus' example, we know that nothing can be accomplished with violence. So let's forget the finger-pointing and the fighting words and, instead, approach the problem and each other with mutual respect and mutual love for the real victims: our children.

When children kill children, we adults must do what we can to get the guns out of their hands. If we don't do our part, the blood of these children will be on our hands.

EVALUATING THE AUTHOR'S ARGUMENT:

In the viewpoint you just read, Bruce Wellems argues that violent video games and movies encourage children to act violently. Do you agree or disagree? Have you played video games or watched movies that are violent? Do you feel you have been affected by them? Explain your answer.

Gun Control Cannot Prevent School Shootings

Jennifer Freeman

"Blaming inanimate objects is yet another display of failure to accept responsibility."

In the following viewpoint, Jennifer Freeman explains why imposing stricter gun control will not prevent school shootings. According to Freeman, guns are not the problem: It is a dearth of social values that causes school and other societal violence. She maintains that children used to bring firearms to school for Reserve Officers' Training Corps (ROTC) programs and after-school hunting clubs—and these activities did not result in school shootings. Gun violence in schools, concludes Freeman, stems from society's failure to encourage children to be proud of their country and respect their environment.

Jennifer Freeman is the cofounder and executive director of Liberty Belles, an organization committed to protecting the rights of gun owners.

AS YOU READ, CONSIDER THE FOLLOWING QUESTIONS:

1. According to the author, what role does the media play in society's perception of what causes gun violence?

Jennifer Freeman, " Guns Not to Blame in School Shootings," Liberty Belles, www.libertybelles.org , 2005. Reproduced by permission.

2. What negative social trends came out of the 1960s, according to Freeman?

3. Why has Israel not had any school shootings since 1974, in Freeman's view?

T he recent shooting massacre at Red Lake High School [on March 21, 2005, in Minnesota] represents a horrific event that could happen at any school in the United States. Every day we hear additional news stories about children or teenagers who bring firearms to school. In most cases, the firearms are confiscated without incident. This provides little comfort, however, as the very idea of a child having

Heartfelt tributes line the perimeter of Red Lake High School in Minnesota after Jeff Weise killed nine people with his grandfather's guns.

access to a loaded firearm and smuggling it into school without their parents' knowledge is more of a risk than any of us would like to take with our children's lives.

When a shooting does occur at school, you can count on the media to lend a helping-hand to their anti-gun buddies in Congress by isolating the gun as the cause of the crime. The media wants you to view the blood, suffering, and loss and come to the conclusion that the crime never would have occurred if the child did not have a gun.

Kids and Guns Don't Have to End in Violence

What the media blatantly fails to recognize, however, is that teenagers used to bring guns to school on a regular basis at a time when school shootings did not exist.

Firearms were stored at school by students who planned after-school hunting and target shooting activities. The ROTC [Reserve Officers' Training Corps] also used real firearms with live ammunition for decades before they were banned in schools.

This occurred at a time when children obeyed their parents and teachers and respected each other. This type of respect for others and joy of life was displayed in many facets of our culture including books, movies, and music. Children were readily disciplined in an effort to raise them to be responsible adults. Americans in general were proud of their country and anxious to contribute their best.

Failure to Teach Values Results in Violence

Despite the important landmark advances in civil rights and freedom of expression, social values in the United States have changed dramatically since the drug and sex revolution of the 1960's. Many aspects of our culture glorify and encourage personal behavior that often results in feelings of isolation, detachment, and loss of self-respect.

Today, many of America's children are being raised in a culture without any life-affirming, disciplined values to balance out external factors. Parents and teachers are failing to hold children responsible for their actions, leaving them without role models and without expectations of behavior. Many adults relinquish control of their children with disastrous results. In many cases, kids with behavioral problems are being prescribed mood-altering drugs as a means to

Passing on core values through parental involvement and behavior modeling are crucial in preventing teen gun violence.

control behavior without exercising discipline. Very little is being discussed about the violent side-effects of these drugs.

Guns Are Not the Problem

Blaming inanimate objects is yet another display of failure to accept responsibility. There is no telling how many young people are graduating from high school with serious mental issues that will only be further exacerbated once they enter college or the work force. It is imperative that we, as a society, make a concerted effort to identify the root of this problem. This will be difficult to achieve since the very institutions who want to take away our guns contribute greatly to the fragmentation of our society, lack of common culture, and intolerance for life-affirming expressions or behaviors.

It is worth noting here that Israel, a country targeted by terrorists on a daily basis, *has not had a school shooting since 1974.* They eliminated their vulnerability to attack by arming and training teachers and administrators in firearm use. And while this may seem like a shocking suggestion to American teachers, there is no telling how many lives and injuries could have been prevented if the school's administration had taken a more proactive role in providing for the defense of the children.

EVALUATING THE AUTHOR'S ARGUMENT:

In this viewpoint, Jennifer Freeman paints a picture of American society in which people are selfish and disrespectful and fail to take responsibility for their actions. Do you agree with her perception? Why or why not?

Armed Security Guards Can Prevent School Shootings

Jews for the Preservation of Firearms Ownership

"Help your fellow American understand: 'gun control' kills."

The following viewpoint was taken from the Web site of Jews for the Preservation of Firearms Ownership, a pro-gun group. The authors believe that gun control leaves people unarmed and unable to defend themselves against armed attackers and criminals. They discuss the 2005 Red Lake High School shootings and argue that had the security guards been able to carry guns, they could have prevented the murder of teachers and students. Gun control, they conclude, allows school shooters to gain the upper hand against unarmed teachers and students.

AS YOU READ, CONSIDER THE FOLLOWING QUESTIONS:

1. In the opinion of the authors, what two events caused the shooting at Red Lake High School?
2. What three elements make the Red Lake High School shooting similar to other mass killings, according to the authors?
3. What did Jeff Weise do before he went to the high school, as reported by the article?

*I*magine that you are a new security guard in a school known for troubled teens and violence. From your office window you see a student step out of a truck and fire two shotgun blasts into the air. Wearing a long black trenchcoat opened to reveal more weapons, the student carrying the shotgun approaches your office.

Visions of the worst possible scenario—Columbine—blink in your mind. You must protect the students. You must act.

Hellish Moments, Deadly Results

But you are unarmed. Your security guard partner is unarmed as well. You have no bullet-proof vest. You deploy your only defensive tactic: radio for help.

The attacker looks into your office windows, searches for the door, finds it, enters and fires the gun. You shout at your partner to run away with you, but instead he stalls the attacker a few seconds. You run out the door. Two shotgun blasts later, your partner is dead.

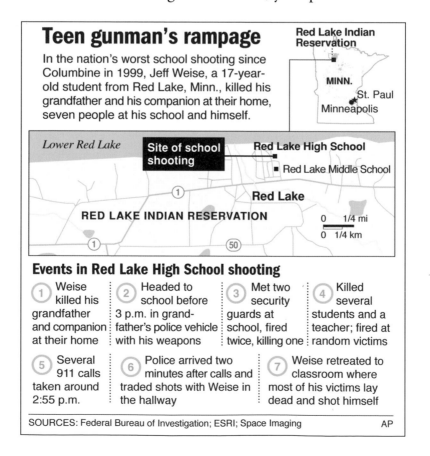

Teen gunman's rampage

Red Lake Indian Reservation

In the nation's worst school shooting since Columbine in 1999, Jeff Weise, a 17-year-old student from Red Lake, Minn., killed his grandfather and his companion at their home, seven people at his school and himself.

MINN.
St. Paul
Minneapolis

Lower Red Lake

Site of school shooting

Red Lake High School
■ Red Lake Middle School

① **Red Lake**

RED LAKE INDIAN RESERVATION

0   1/4 mi
0   1/4 km

① ㊿

Events in Red Lake High School shooting

① Weise killed his grandfather and companion at their home

② Headed to school before 3 p.m. in grandfather's police vehicle with his weapons

③ Met two security guards at school, fired twice, killing one

④ Killed several students and a teacher; fired at random victims

⑤ Several 911 calls taken around 2:55 p.m.

⑥ Police arrived two minutes after calls and traded shots with Weise in the hallway

⑦ Weise retreated to classroom where most of his victims lay dead and shot himself

SOURCES: Federal Bureau of Investigation; ESRI; Space Imaging   AP

You shout to students to run away, and many do run away with you. The attacker enters a classroom, kills the teacher and several students, and grievously wounds many others. One brave student, who tries to fight the attacker by wrestling with him and stabbing him with a pencil, is shot and gravely injured.

Hellish moments, deadly results. You won't forget those flashing seconds or the faces of the dead. Ever.

The Presence of Guns Protects

Every word of this story is true, according to press reports. It all happened on Monday, March 21, 2005, at Red Lake High School in Minnesota. The security guard on duty was a 20-year-old woman with two young children at home. Her partner, Derrick Brun, was 28.

No question: this was a security failure catastrophe. Two causes combined: (1) An armed attacker with a plan to kill, and (2) a "security team" that was unarmed, unprotected, and incapable of defending against this well-known possible threat.

Why were the security guards *unarmed* at Red Lake High School? Because of "gun control" ideas. Somebody at Red Lake believed the lies that "you're more likely to be killed if you resist with a gun" and "the presence of guns causes violence."

Somebody at Red Lake consciously took these actions:

- Hired two young security guards
- Assured the guards were powerless to protect the students, teachers and themselves against armed attackers
- Told the students, teachers and parents that the school would be "safer" with two unarmed security guards, rather than two armed guards.

That "somebody" ignored the post-Columbine warnings against laws and policies that guarantee schools are defense-free zones. That "somebody" deserves a lifetime of chilling nightmares and profound regrets.

Gun Control Leaves the Wrong People Unarmed

The mass killing at Red Lake High School followed the pattern of 20th-century genocides—the same three crucial elements appear in each case: (1) an evil idea to kill innocents, (2) a systematic program

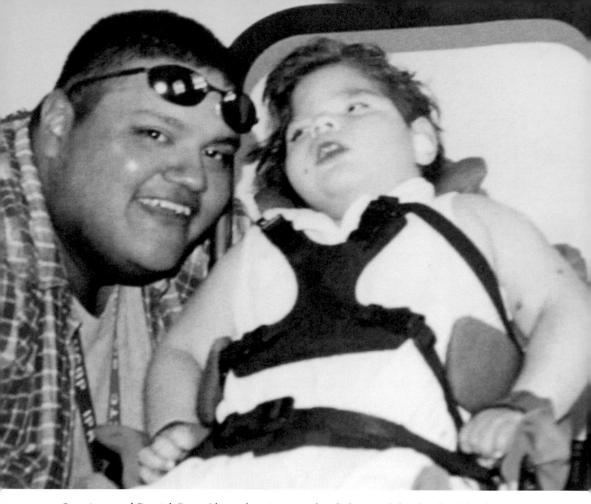

Security guard Derrick Brun (shown here in an undated photo with his daughter) lost his life when Jeff Weise opened fire at Red Lake High School.

of rendering the victims unarmed and undefended, and (3) the betrayal of trust.

In national genocides, the government disarms the victims using various "gun control" schemes. The victims continue to trust the government to protect them and not to kill them, so the victims comply with the "gun control." The government betrays that trust and murders the victims.

At Red Lake, the killer hatched the evil plan to murder. He killed his grandfather, a police officer, and took weapons. The government had prepared the way for him to kill his next victims by assuring, via "gun control" policies, that nobody at the high school was armed. Despite the recent history of school shootings by armed students, the authorities had successfully convinced the victims to rely upon the school's unarmed security guard plan. The victims believed the authorities and trusted that they were "safe." When the armed attacker came to school, the victims' trust was betrayed—the security plan was guaranteed to fail—and many victims suffered severe injuries and death. . . .

An Unarmed Citizenry Is a Defenseless One

From the Armenian Genocide to the Nazi Holocaust to the Rwanda Genocide to the Luby's Cafeteria killings to the 9/11 disaster, the same factors play out. And now again at Red Lake High School.

Help your fellow American understand: "gun control" kills.

If we gun owners fail to communicate this message, then Red Lake, like Columbine, will be added as a bogus justification to register, ban, and confiscate firearms nationwide. We have a choice: either we respond powerfully to the anti-defense propaganda storm, or we surrender our rights and our guns.

EVALUATING THE AUTHOR'S ARGUMENT:

In this viewpoint, the authors argue that gun control laws contributed to the murders at Red Lake High School and other schools. What do you think? Would arming school security guards increase or decrease school violence? Use evidence from the viewpoints in this chapter to support your answer.

Viewpoint
4

Armed Security Guards Cannot Prevent School Shootings

"We must look deeper for a solution than just superficial security measures such as cameras and guards."

Randy Poindexter

Author Randy Poindexter contends in the following viewpoint that extra security measures such as armed guards are useless without first understanding why school violence happens. Resources must be spent on understanding and anticipating school violence rather than on simply reacting to it, he claims.

Randy Poindexter is the executive vice president of the National Institute for School and Workplace Safety (NISWS), a consulting company in Florida that works with schools to develop and increase safety programs.

AS YOU READ, CONSIDER THE FOLLOWING QUESTIONS:

1. According to the author, what is the name of the process that studies random acts of targeted violence?

2. What components make up a Safe School Plan, in the opinion of Poindexter?

3. Explain the importance to the author's argument of four of the six findings of the Secret Service, as described in the viewpoint.

Randy Poindexter, "Red Lake Shootings: Predictable or Preventable?" National Institute for School and Workplace Safety, www.nisws.com, 2005. Reproduced with permission,

We have all watched and listened to the news with heavy hearts as the story unfolds of another senseless and tragic school shooting, this time in northern Minnesota [on March 21, 2005]. We mourn and grieve for the lives lost and the families and friends of the victims.

The shooter is alleged to be 16 year old Jeff Weise who allegedly killed four adults and five students before taking his own life. The victims included Weise's grandfather and the grandfather's friend, a security guard at Red Lake High School, a teacher at the school, and five students at the school. Several other students at the school were wounded and at least two are critical.

We Need Meaningful Security Measures

Now we are all left to wonder how another act of targeted violence of this magnitude could occur after America's schools have implemented so many security measures in the past few years. Red Lake High School had an unarmed security guard at the front entrance manning the metal detector and security cameras throughout the

© Fairington, 03/05, Cagle Cartoons

school. There were other security measures in place at the school, so perhaps we must look deeper for a solution than just superficial security measures such as cameras and guards. While these actions are extremely important for school security, they are only one part of a complete Safe School Plan.

The United States Secret Service worked with The United States Department of Education a few years ago to study random acts of targeted violence in America's schools after the proliferation of school shootings in the 1990's. They used a process called Threat Assessment to study 37 different school shootings and interviewed many of the shooters themselves to try to gather information that may help school administrators better understand these acts of targeted violence and why they occur. The results of the U.S. Secret Service study were ultimately published to better help school administrators and law enforcement officials work together to develop Safe School Plans to prevent violence from occurring.

Components of Good Response Plans

It is important to differentiate that most schools now have an Emergency Response Plan to deal with a crisis after it occurs, but few have a Safe School Plan which includes components for prevention/intervention, preparedness, response and recovery for multi-hazard threats and terrorism before they occur.

Look for the Signs of the Potential for Violence

Some of the Secret Service findings that apply here include:

1. **Incidents of targeted violence are rarely sudden, impulsive acts.**

   Jeff Weise didn't just suddenly "snap" and start killing people. This was a discernable, well-thought-out plan in advance of the attack.

2. **Prior to most incidents, other people knew about the attacker's ideas and plans.**

   Jeff Weise had shown drawings and writings to other students depicting killings, school shootings and suicide. Some students had even commented that these drawings and writings about the killings appeared to be about Red Lake High School.

3. **Most attackers engage in some behavior, prior to the incident, that caused others concern or indicated a need for help.**

   Jeff Weise had long been known to be associated with anti-social extremist groups and had an extensive discipline record at the school. In fact, he had been removed from the school and assigned a home tutoring program. He had engaged in internet chat groups which encourage hatred and prejudice. While many times he used a fictitious screen name, often times he used his real name and even identified himself as a student at Red Lake High School. Many students and teachers had expressed concern about his behavior.

4. **Most attackers had difficulty coping with significant losses or personal failures.**

   Jeff Weiss's father committed suicide several years ago and his mother was critically injured in an automobile accident which killed his cousin. His mother remains institutionalized in a "vegetative state" to this day. Jeff was badly abused by both his father and mother when he was a child.

5. **Most attackers felt bullied or persecuted by others before the attack.**

   Jeff Weise was a victim of bullying at school because of his anti-social behavior. He was a "loner and outcast" with few or no friends. He was constantly teased and tormented about his dress and his anti-social behavior.

6. **Most attackers had access to weapons prior to the attack.**

   The grandfather of Jeff Weise was a law enforcement officer and had several guns at home. Jeff had access to and used his grandfather's guns for all of the shootings at Red Lake High School.

Warning Signs Are Best Defense

This is a classic case of targeted violence that fits the Secret Service findings in their study of school shootings. ***While there are no useful*** *profiles of school shooters, there are many early warning signs that, if noticed and acted upon, can prevent school violence!*

It is imperative that school administrators become familiar with the Threat Assessment Model and train their faculty and staff to identify early warning signs that indicate a student may be at risk of causing violence or being the victim of a violent act.

"In the wake of almost every disastrous event, when the pieces are put together, we discover that we had enough information to deal with the problem in advance, if only . . ."

—"The Gift of Fear"
Gavin DeBecker

EVALUATING THE AUTHOR'S ARGUMENT:

In this viewpoint, the author maintains that school violence can be prevented if school officials learn about what causes a student to become violent. Do you agree? Can society ever understand what motivates school shooters enough to prevent them? Explain your reasoning.

Facts About Gun Control

Guns in America

According to the Centers for Disease Control and Prevention:

- 11,920 Americans were killed with a firearm in 2003
- 16,907 Americans committed suicide with a firearm in 2003
- Firearms are the second leading cause of injury deaths, after motor vehicle traffic injuries
- Men are six times more likely than women to die from a firearm-related injury
- African Americans are twice as likely as whites to die from a firearm-related injury

According to Gallup's 2005 crime survey:

- There are approximately 200 million guns in the United States
- Four in ten Americans have a gun in their home
- Thirty percent of Americans own a gun
- Twelve percent of Americans report that a gun is owned by someone else in the household
- Gun owners report that they use their guns to protect themselves from crime and for target shooting and hunting
- Americans living in the Midwest and the South are more likely to own a gun than those who live in the East and the West
- Thirty-three percent of whites and 18 percent of nonwhites report owning a gun

Gun Control Laws in America

According to the Brady Campaign to Prevent Gun Violence's 2005 State Report Cards:

- California, Maryland, South Carolina, and Virginia limit the purchase of handguns to one per person in a thirty-day period
- California, Connecticut, Delaware, Florida, Hawaii, Illinois, Kansas, Maine, Massachusetts, Minnesota, New Hampshire, New Jersey, North Carolina, Rhode Island, Texas, Virginia, Wisconsin, and Washington, D.C., have Child Access Prevention

(CAP) laws, which hold gun owners responsible for leaving guns accessible to children
- Forty-one states do not require firearms to be registered with law enforcement agencies
- Assault weapons must be registered in California, Connecticut, Maryland, and New Jersey
- It is illegal to own a firearm without a license in Illinois and Massachusetts, but there are no state registration requirements
- Only handguns have to be registered in New York and Michigan
- Fifteen states (California, Connecticut, Hawaii, Illinois, Iowa, Maryland, Massachusetts, Michigan, Missouri, Nebraska, New Jersey, New Mexico, New York, North Carolina, and Rhode Island) require a license in order to purchase a handgun
- Only California, Connecticut, Hawaii, Maryland, Massachusetts, Michigan, and Rhode Island require safety training for handgun buyers

Guns and Women
- It is estimated that between 11 million and 17 million American women own guns
- According to the National Rifle Association, approximately 2 million American women hunt, and another 4 million use a gun for target shooting

According to a 2005 Gallup poll:
- Women are less likely to own a gun than are men—just 13 percent of women own a gun, compared with 47 percent of men
- Seventy-four percent of female gun owners use their gun for protection, as opposed to 63 percent of male gun owners

A 2005 *USA Today*/CNN/Gallup poll found that:
- More women than men (53 percent vs. 34 percent) believe that only government safety officials should be allowed to carry concealed firearms
- Twenty-six percent of women believe that citizens with a clear need should be permitted to carry a concealed weapon
- Seventeen percent of women think any citizen should be able to carry a concealed firearm

Guns and Children

According to the Rand Corporation:

- Thirty-four percent of children in America live in homes with at least one firearm—that is more than 22 million children
- There is more than one firearm in 69 percent of homes that have both children and firearms
- Approximately 13 percent of homes that have children and firearms (or 2.6 million children in 1.4 million homes) store firearms in ways that are accessible to children

According to the *Juvenile Offenders and Victims: 2006 National Report*, published by the National Center for Juvenile Justice:

- Half of the 46,600 children aged seventeen and younger who were murdered between 1980 and 2002 were killed with a firearm
- Seventy-eight percent of children between the ages of fifteen and seventeen who were murdered between 1980 and 2002 were killed with a firearm
- Twice as many boys as girls were killed with a firearm between 1980 and 2002
- Between 1981 and 2001, 60 percent of all children who committed suicide used a firearm

The Children's Defense Fund reports that in 2003:

- More children were killed by firearms in California, Texas, Illinois, New York, Pennsylvania, Florida, and North Carolina than in other states
- Hawaii, Vermont, New Hampshire, Rhode Island, North Dakota, Maine, and South Dakota had the smallest number of children killed by firearms

According to the Centers for Disease Control and Prevention's 2005 Youth Risk Behavior Surveillance:

- Of the 18.5 percent of middle and high school students across the United States who reported bringing a weapon (such as a gun or knife) to school on more than one day in the thirty days before the survey was taken, 5.4 percent said they carried a gun
- More boys (9.9 percent) than girls (0.9 percent) said they carried a gun to school on more than one day in the thirty days before the survey was taken

- More white (9.7 percent), African American (9.4 percent), and Hispanic (11.6 percent) male students reported carrying a gun to school than did white (0.9 percent), African American (0.9 percent), and Hispanic (0 percent) female students

The Uhlich Children's Advantage Network's 2005 National Teen Gun Survey found that:

- More than 82 percent of teens think that handguns should be childproofed just as medicine bottles are childproofed
- More than 10 percent of teens believe that principals and teachers should be allowed to bring handguns to school to protect students
- More than 68 percent of American teenagers believe there are too many guns in society
- The proportion of teens who believe they will be shot one day is 39 percent
- The proportion of teenagers who feel that gun violence will erupt in their school is 35.9 percent

Glossary

assault weapon: A semiautomatic gun that can include such items as an attachment for a bayonet, a folding stock that allows the weapon to be stored, and an ammunition magazine that can hold many rounds of ammunition.

background check: When a licensed gun dealer checks the background of a person wanting to buy a gun to ensure the person is legally allowed to own a gun. A person who is a convicted felon, has a history of mental instability, or has an outstanding restraining order is not allowed to own a gun.

Brady law: Signed into law in 1993, it requires a five-day waiting period and background check on handgun purchases.

Bureau of Alcohol, Tobacco, Firearms and Explosives (ATF): Government organization responsible for reducing violent crime and enforcing federal gun laws.

Child Access Prevention (CAP) laws: Also known as "safe storage laws," the laws generally require that adults use gun locks or store loaded firearms in a place that children cannot reach. The adult is criminally liable if a child gets hold of a loaded gun that has not been stored properly.

concealed weapon: A firearm small enough to be carried out of view.

concealed-carry weapon (CCW) permits: Licenses that allow an individual to carry a concealed weapon in public.

gun control: Efforts to reduce the availability and use of firearms.

handgun: A gun that can be fired from one hand, has a barrel less than sixteen inches long, and can be concealed on the person.

justifiable homicide: Killing another person without intent, such as killing someone in self-defense to protect oneself or someone else.

militia: A fighting force put together from a community or state that often serves only in emergency situations.

personalized or "smart gun": A handgun that can be programmed to recognize only the owner or an authorized user and prevent anyone else from firing it.

Project ChildSafe: Supported by the U.S. Department of Justice and managed by National Shooting Sports Foundation, the program publicizes the safe handling and storage of firearms by distributing free gun-lock kits and safety-education material.

Protection of Lawful Commerce in Arms Act: Signed into law on October 26, 2005, the law protects gun manufacturers and retailers from being sued by victims of gun violence.

semiautomatic weapon: A firearm that automatically puts a bullet into the firing chamber each time the trigger is squeezed, allowing the shooter to fire continuously without stopping to reload manually.

"stand your ground" law: A law allowing a person to use deadly force in a public place if he or she feels threatened with violence or an attack. Challenges the previously held idea that the person who is being attacked has a duty to retreat (that the person should avoid violence if it is reasonably possible to escape from the attacker). As of July 2006, ten states had "stand your ground" laws and thirteen others were considering them.

trigger lock: A device that prevents the trigger of a firearm from being pulled and accidentally discharging the gun.

waiting periods: These provide time for a background check to be finished before a firearm can be purchased.

Organizations to Contact

American Civil Liberties Union (ACLU)
125 Broad St., 18th Fl.
New York, NY 10004
(212) 549-2500
e-mail: aclu@aclu.org
Web site: www.aclu.org

The ACLU champions the rights set forth in the Declaration of Independence and the U.S. Constitution. It interprets the Second Amendment as a guarantee for states to form militias, not as a guarantee of the individual right to own and bear firearms. Consequently, the organization believes that gun control is constitutional and necessary.

Americans for Gun Safety (AGS)
Washington, DC
(202) 775-0300
Web sites: www.americansforgunsafety.com
www.agsfoundation.com

The organization supports the rights of law-abiding people to own guns. AGS supports such measures as background checks at gun shows, gun safety measures for children, and enforcing laws banning illegal gun trafficking.

The Brady Center to Prevent Handgun Violence
1225 I St. NW, Suite 1100
Washington, DC 20005
(202) 289-7319
fax: (202) 408-1851
Web sites: www.cphv.org • www.gunlawsuits.org

The center is the legal action, research, and education affiliate of Handgun Control, Inc. The center's Legal Action Project provides free legal representation for victims in lawsuits against reckless gun manufacturers, dealers, and owners.

Canadian Coalition for Gun Control

PO Box 90062, 1488 Queen St. W.
Toronto, ON M6K 3K3
(416) 604-0209
Web site: www.guncontrol.ca

The coalition was formed to reduce gun death, injury, and crime. It supports the registration of all guns and works for tougher restrictions on handguns. The organization promotes safe storage requirements for all firearms and educates to counter the romance of guns. Various fact sheets and other education materials on gun control are available on its Web site.

Citizens Committee for the Right to Keep and Bear Arms

12500 NE Tenth Pl.
Bellevue, WA 98005
(425) 454-491
Web site: www.ccrkba.org

The committee believes that the U.S. Constitution's Second Amendment guarantees and protects the right of individual Americans to own guns. It works to educate the public concerning this right and to lobby legislators to prevent the passage of gun control laws.

Coalition to Stop Gun Violence

1023 Fifteenth St. NW, Suite 301
Washington, DC 20005
(202) 408-0061
Web site: www.csgv.org

The coalition lobbies at the local, state, and federal levels to ban the sale of handguns and assault weapons to individuals and to institute licensing and registration of all firearms. It also litigates cases against firearms makers.

Doctors for Responsible Gun Ownership

The Claremont Institute
937 W. Foothill Blvd., Suite E
Claremont, CA 91711

(909) 621-6825
Web site: www.claremont.org

The organization consists of health professionals familiar with guns and medical research. It works to correct poor medical scholarship about the dangers of guns and to educate people on the importance of guns for self-defense. The organization has legally challenged laws that regulate guns.

Gun Owners of America (GOA)
8001 Forbes Pl., Suite 102
Springfield, VA 22151
(703) 321-8585
e-mail: goamail@gunowners.org
Web sites: www.gunowners.org
www.gunowners.com

This lobbying organization supports the ownership of guns as an issue of personal freedom and is dedicated to protecting and defending the Second Amendment rights of gun owners. Its online resources include the newsletter the *Gunowners*, gun control fact sheets, and information about firearms legislation in Congress.

Independence Institute
13952 Denver West Pkwy., Suite 400
Golden, CO 80401
(303) 279-6536
Web site: www.i2i.org

The Independence Institute is a think tank that supports gun ownership as a civil liberty and a constitutional right. Its publications include articles and booklets opposing gun control, many of which are found on its Web site.

Jews for the Preservation of Firearms Ownership (JPFO)
PO Box 270143
Hartford, WI 53027
(262) 673-9745
e-mail: jpfo@jpfo.org
Web site: www.jpfo.org

JPFO is an organization that believes Jewish law mandates self-defense. Its primary goal is the elimination of the idea that gun control is a socially useful public policy.

Join Together
One Appleton St., 4th Fl.
Boston, MA 02116-5223
(617) 437-1500
e-mail: info@jointogether.org
Web site: www.jointogether.org

Join Together, a project of the Boston University School of Public Health, is an organization that serves as a national resource for communities working to reduce substance abuse and gun violence.

Million Mom March
1225 I St. NW, Suite 1100
Washington, DC 20005
(888) 989-MOMS
Web site: www.millionmommarch.org

The foundation is a grassroots organization that supports common sense gun laws. The foundation organized the Million Mom March, in which thousands marched through Washington, D.C., on Mother's Day, May 14, 2000, in support of licensing, registration, and other firearms regulations.

National Crime Prevention Council (NCPC)
1000 Connecticut Ave. NW, 13th Fl.
Washington, DC 20036
(202) 466-6272
Web site: www.ncpc.org

The NCPC is a branch of the U.S. Department of Justice. Through its programs and education materials, the council works to teach Americans how to reduce crime and to address its causes. It provides readers with information on gun control and gun violence.

National Rifle Association of America (NRA)
11250 Waples Mill Rd.

Fairfax, VA 22030
(703) 267-1000
Web site: www.nra.org

With nearly 3 million members, the NRA is America's largest organization of gun owners. The NRA believes that gun control laws violate the U.S. Constitution and do not reduce crime.

Second Amendment Foundation

12500 NE Tenth Pl.
Bellevue, WA 98005
(425) 454-7012
Web site: www.saf.org

The foundation is dedicated to informing Americans about their Second Amendment right to keep and bear firearms. The foundation publishes numerous books, including *The Best Defense: True Stories of Intended Victims Who Defended Themselves with a Firearm*, and *CCW: Carrying Concealed Weapons*. The complete text of the book *How to Defend Your Gun Rights* is available on its Web site.

Violence Policy Center

1730 Rhode Island Ave. NW, Suite 1014
Washington, DC 20036
(202) 822-8200
e-mail: info@vpc.org
Web site: www.vpc.org

The center is an educational foundation that conducts research on firearms violence. It works to educate the public concerning the dangers of guns and supports gun control measures. The center's publications include the reports *Safe at Home: How DC's Gun Laws Save Children's Lives; An Analysis of the Decline in Gun Dealers, 1994 to 2005*; and *Really Big Guns, Even Bigger Lies*.

For Further Reading

Books

Sarah Brady and Merrill McLoughlin, *A Good Fight*. New York: Public Affairs, 2002. Written by the wife of Jim Brady, who was injured in the assassination attempt on President Reagan in 1981, this story recounts her fight to pass the Brady bill, which became law in 1993, and her mission to reduce gun violence.

Peter Harry Brown and Daniel G. Abel, *Outgunned: Up Against the NRA; The First Complete Insider Account of the Battle over Gun Control*. New York: Free Press, 2003. Explores the battle between the National Rifle Association and gun control advocates over gun control legislation.

Gregg Lee Carter, ed., *Gun Control in the United States: A Reference Handbook*. Santa Barbara, CA: ABC-CLIO, 2006. Provides an overview of gun control in America, including the history of gun control, key legislation and its effectiveness, court decisions, and a comparison of U.S. gun control laws with those of other countries.

Saul Cornell, *A Well-Regulated Militia: The Founding Fathers and the Origin of Gun Control in America*. New York: Oxford University Press, 2006. The author discusses the debate over the interpretation of the Second Amendment, which Cornell contends was intended to mean that citizens were obligated to keep and bear arms in order to take part in a well-regulated militia.

Wendy Cukier and Victor W. Sidel, *The Global Gun Epidemic: From Saturday Night Specials to AK-47s*. Westport, CT: Praeger Security International, 2006. Examines gun violence as a worldwide problem, including how that violence affects societies, how firearms are obtained both legally and illegally, and ways in which gun violence can be reduced.

Donna Dees-Thomases, *Looking for a Few Good Moms: How One Mother Rallied a Million Others Against the Gun Lobby*. New York: Rodale, 2004. Written by the founder of the Million Mom March, which was organized in response to gun violence and to lobby Congress for stronger gun control laws, this book describes how the organization took root and evolved.

David Hemenway, *Private Guns, Public Health*. Ann Arbor: University of Michigan Press, 2004. A professor of health policy argues that gun violence can be reduced by treating it as a public health issue, just as cigarette smoking and drunk driving are.

Caitlin Kelly, *Blown Away: American Women and Guns*. New York: Pocket, 2004. An examination of guns and women, including why some women will own a firearm, why some refuse to own one, women who have been affected by gun violence, and how society views women and guns.

Abigail A. Kohn, *Shooters: Myths and Realities of America's Gun Cultures*. New York: Oxford University Press, 2004. Discusses the attitudes and misconceptions Americans have about guns and examines why gun rights advocates own guns.

David B. Kopel, Stephen P. Halbrook, and Alan Korwin, *Supreme Court Gun Cases*. Phoenix, AZ: Bloomfield, 2003. The authors argue for gun ownership by examining the number of cases involving firearms that were brought before the Supreme Court in which the Court recognized the rights of individuals to own guns.

Wayne R. LaPierre and James Jay Baker, *Shooting Straight: Telling the Truth About Guns in America*. Washington, DC: Regnery, 2002. The authors argue that gun regulation increases crime and violence.

John R. Lott Jr., *The Bias Against Guns*. Washington, DC: Regnery, 2003. The author maintains that the anti-gun media present a one-sided view of guns and neglect to examine the role that guns can play in preventing crime and violence.

Jens Ludwig and Philip J. Cook, eds., *Evaluating Gun Policy: Effects on Crime and Violence*. Washington, DC: Brookings Institution, 2003. Examines the connection between gun ownership and violence.

Jack Reynolds, *A People Armed and Free: The Truth About the Second Amendment*. Bloomington, IN: AuthorHouse, 2003. Analyzes the meaning of the Second Amendment, how it applies to an individual's right to own a gun, and recent gun rights legislation.

Robert J. Spitzer, *The Politics of Gun Control*. Washington, DC: CQ Press, 2004. The third edition of an examination of the positions of gun control advocates and opponents and how these positions have been changed by recent school shootings and the terrorist attacks on September 11, 2001.

Periodicals and Reports

America's Intelligence Wire, "Kansas State University: Weapons May Provide Safety for Vulnerable Women," February 14, 2005.

Arkansas Business, "The Gun Ban," September 20, 2004.

Kris Axtman and Mark Clayton, "Guns in the Trunk: Workers Right or Workplace Danger? NRA and Employers Square Off over Oklahoma Law That Allows the Practice," *Christian Science Monitor,* August 12, 2005.

Gerald Bepko, "Do Guns Create or Prevent Violence?" *Indianapolis Business Journal,* October 11, 2004.

Buffalo (NY) News, "The Canadian Solution: Register Each and Every Firearm," June 16, 2005.

Sam Chaltain and Molly McCloskey, "Red Lake Shooting: No More Quick Fixes," *USA Today,* March 30, 2005.

Steve Chapman, "A Pointless Ban on Handguns," *Chicago Tribune,* November 13, 2005.

Charlotte (NC) Observer, "Save the Children: North Carolina Faces Point-Blank Need for Gun Safety Campaign," December 30, 2005.

Christian Century, "Middle Ground Elusive on Gun-Control Issue," May 3, 2005.

Philip Cohen, "American Tales of Guns and Ignorance," *New Scientist,* December 25, 2004–January 1, 2005.

Wendy Cukier, "Changing Public Policy on Firearms: Success Stories from Around the World," *Journal of Public Health Policy,* 2005.

Richard M. Daley, "Give Reasonable Gun Laws a Shot," *Chicago Tribune,* March 12, 2004.

Brian Doherty, "A Glorious Sunset," *Reason,* July 15, 2004.

Merle English, "A Woman's Crusade to Stop Gun Violence," *Newsday,* January 8, 2006.

Essence, "Moms March On: 'People Always Say It's Not Guns That Kill, It's People Who Kill.' But If People Can't Get the Guns, They Can't Shoot Anybody," April 2004.

Dianne Feinstein, "Gun Profits for Votes: It's Enough to Make You Sick," *Los Angeles Times*, September 10, 2004.

Bernard E. Harcourt, "Nazi Laws Are a Poor Guide," *National Law Journal*, July 5, 2004.

Gene Healy, "Less Guns, More Crime," *American Spectator*, January 20, 2004.

Spencer S. Hsu, "House Votes to Repeal D.C. Gun Restriction: Measure Would Curb Law That Requires Arms Kept at Home to Be Non-operating," *Washington Post*, July 1, 2005.

Rachel Jurado, "Gun Control Victims," *American Enterprise*, January/February 2004.

Don B. Kates Jr., "More Guns Do Not Mean More Murder," *Handguns*, February/March 2005.

Bob Kemper, "Violence Fails to Raise Gun Control Volume," *Atlanta Journal-Constitution*, April 8, 2005.

Abigail A. Kohn, "The War Against Gun Owners," *American Enterprise*, June 2005.

Abigail A. Kohn, Don B. Kates, Wendy Kaminer, and Michael I. Krauss, "Straight Shooting on Gun Control: A *Reason* Debate," *Reason*, May 2005.

Nicholas D. Kristof, "Lock and Load," *New York Times*, November 13, 2004.

Robert W. Lee, "Defending the Home," *New American*, March 22, 2004.

Juliet Leftwich, "Americans Must Work for State, Local Reform of Firearms Laws," *San Francisco Daily Journal*, December 2, 2004.

John R. Lott Jr., "Assault Weapons Ban Was Useless Anyway," *Los Angeles Times*, September 10, 2004.

———, "City's Assault-Weapons Ban Ineffective and Unneeded," *Columbus (OH) Dispatch*, July 20, 2005.

Joyce Lee Malcolm, "Self-Defense: An Endangered Right," *Cato Policy Report*, March/April 2004.

Zell Miller, "Firearms Firms Need Protection," *Boston Globe*, July 29, 2005.

Courtland Milloy, "So Many Guns in the Hands of Children," *Washington Post*, March 10, 2004.

David Morton, "Gunning for the World," *Foreign Policy*, January/ February 2006.

New American, "From Gun Control to Bullet Control," June 13, 2005.

Josie Newman, "In Toronto, New Crime-Fighting Tactics: Handgun Shootings, Mainly Among Young Black Males in Gangs, Increased Sharply in 2005," *Christian Science Monitor*, December 27, 2005.

Mara Osman, "Taking the Middle Road," *NEA Today*, January 2004.

John Rosenthal, "Make Federal Laws to Reduce Gun Access," *Boston Globe*, January 7, 2006.

Joan Ryan, "Guns Are a Bad Idea, but So Is Ban," *San Francisco Chronicle*, December 23, 3004.

Jim Spencer, "Gun Law Targets Public Data," *Denver Post*, July 21, 2004.

Mike Thomas, "Self-Defense Law Won't Stir Trigger-Mania," *Orlando Sentinel*, October 2, 2005.

Russ Thurman, "Targeting Crime, Not Guns Works to Reduce Gun Violence," *Shooting Industry*, March 2004.

Andrew Trotter, "Schools Wrestle with Issue of Armed Guards," *Education Week News*, April 6, 2005.

Noel Weyrich, "Shooting Blanks," *Philadelphia Magazine*, July 2004.

Richard Williams, "Shooting: Why Britain's Shooters Should Stop Whining About Pistol Ban," *Guardian* (Manchester), January 17, 2006.

Kurt Williamsen, "Protecting Gun Makers from Lawsuits," *New American*, November 28, 2005.

Internet Sources

The Brady Campaign to Prevent Gun Violence, "2005 Gun Violence Prevention Report Cards," 2005. www.bradycampaign.org.

Dick Dahl, "The 'Public Health' Approach to Guns: A Changed Landscape," Join Together, December 23, 2004. www.jointogether.org/ gv/news/features/print/0,2060,575483,00.html.

GunCite, "Original Intent and Purpose of the Second Amendment," October 31, 2004. www.guncite.com.

The HELP Network, "U.S. Firearm Homicide and Suicide Facts," January 20, 2005. www.helpnetwork.org.

Scott McPherson, "Britain's Gun-Control Folly," The Future of Freedom Foundation, 2005. www.fff.org.

Morbidity and Mortality Weekly Report (MMWR), "First Reports Evaluating the Effectiveness of Strategies for Preventing Violence: Firearms Law," Centers for Disease Control and Prevention, 2003. www.cdc.gov/mmwr.

National Rifle Association-Institute for Legislative Action, "The Top 10 Reasons the Clinton Gun Ban Was Allowed to Expire," 2004. www.nraila.org.

National School Safety Center, "School Crime and Violence Statistics," January 2006. www.nssc1.org.

Erich Pratt, "Gun Banners Shooting Themselves in the Foot," *Intellectual Conservative*, 2005. www.intellectualconservative.com.

U.S. Government Accounting Office, "Gun Control and Terrorism: FBI Could Better Manage Firearm-Related Background Checks Involving Terrorist Watch List Records," 2005. www.gao.gov.

Violence Policy Center, "Safe at Home: How D.C.'s Gun Laws Save Children's Lives," July 2005. www.vpc.org.

Web Sites

Bureau of Alcohol, Tobacco, Firearms and Explosives, U.S. Department of Justice (www.atf.gov/firearms/index.htm). A law enforcement agency within the U.S. Department of Justice, the goals of the Bureau of Alcohol, Tobacco, Firearms and Explosives are to reduce violent crime and prevent terrorism. The Web site contains research, information, publications about state and federal firearm laws and regulations, and statistics, including crimes involving young people, illegal gun trafficking, and firearms traced to crimes.

Jurist, The Legal Education Network: Gun Laws, Gun Control, and Gun Rights (http://jurist.law.pitt.edu/gunlaw.htm). A legal news and legal research program of the University of Pittsburgh School of Law, the Web site offers an extensive overview about gun laws, control, and rights.

Project ChildSafe (www.projectchildsafe.org). Project ChildSafe is a nationwide program supported by the U.S. Department of Justice and managed by the National Shooting Sports Foundation, which is devoted to promoting the safe handling and storage of firearms. The resources on the Web site include information on teaching children what to do if they find a gun, different methods for safely storing a firearm, and how to obtain a free firearm safety kit.

The Second Amendment Research Center (www.secondamendment-center.org). Based at the John Glenn Institute for Public Service and Public Policy at Ohio State University, the center's goals are to examine how gun violence can be reduced while protecting the rights of gun owners. The Web site is an excellent resource that includes a listing of articles by experts on both sides of the issue.

Index

Picture Credits

Cover, © Mark Peterson/CORBIS
Associated Press, AP, 11, 24, 31, 32, 49, 50, 60, 65, 66, 75, 80, 82
© Najlah Feanney/CORBIS, 68
© Scott Houston/SYGMA/CORBIS, 43
© Reuters/CORBIS, 36
© Royalty Free/CORBIS, 13
© Steve Starr/CORBIS, 10
© Tom Stewart/CORBIS, 77
© Les Stone/SYGMA/CORBIS, 21
Getty Images, 45
Steve Zmina, 15, 34, 39, 55, 71

About the Editor

Beth Rosenthal has been in publishing for the last 18 years. She has worked as a copy editor, proofreader, researcher, project manager, and permissions associate for a variety of medical, health care, parenting, and business publications and Web sites. A freelance editor for the last five years, Beth lives with her husband, two daughters, and a cat on the East Coast.